April 1992

"Good company in a journey makes the way seem

Izaak Walton.

Thanks for your friendship Sulebha. Looking forward to some great adventures in South Africa together.
Love Silvia

The Scenic Splendours of Southern Africa

The Scenic Splendours of Southern Africa

Text by David Bristow
Photographs by Gerald Cubitt

Struik

Struik Publishers
an operating division of The Struik Group (Pty) Ltd

Struik House
Oswald Pirow Street
Foreshore
Cape Town

Reg. No. 80/02842/07

First Published 1988

Editors: Ellis Pender and Desireé Doran
Design and typography: Neville Poulter
Cover design: Tracey Carstens (trade edition)

Typesetting and reproduction by Hirt & Carter (Pty) Ltd, Cape Town
Printing and binding by Printpak Books, Cape

ISBN 0-86977-735-1 (English trade edition)
ISBN 0-86977-845-5 (English PLC edition)

Contents

Half-title page: *The foothills of the Drakensberg mountains in the eastern Orange Free State.*

Title page: *The vast landscapes of Namaqualand, north-western Cape.*

Pages 4-5: *Springbok in the dry bed of the Nossob River, Kalahari Gemsbok National Park.*

Page 6: *Tsitsikamma Coastal National Park, one of South Africa's true wilderness areas.*

Pages 8-9: *A landscape in the vicinity of Van Reenen's Pass, Natal.*

Introduction

This book takes us on a journey, not only through the breathtaking vistas of southern Africa, but also through time, as we witness the workings of nature as it has carved out the landscapes over billions of years. We can also see how the plants and animals have evolved in sympathy with the changing climate and topography, with the soils and shifting wetlands and with each other in a fantastic, slow-motion, genetic choreography.

In all likelihood Man was born in Africa, probably in the gorges of the Rift Valley of East Africa. However, remains of his earlier ancestors *Australopithecus africanus* and *A. robustus*, the first upright primates and toolmakers, have been been found in archaeological sites in southern Africa. But the odyssey we are about to witness takes us back, far beyond the mere several millions of years before man and his primate relatives first appeared. On close observation, the face of southern Africa reveals stories from the oldest rocks on earth, and trapped in them we can also see, in ascending order, fossils of some of the first amphibians and reptiles that colonized the land, and examples of the earliest mammals that evolved from the reptiles.

Today the landscapes of our subcontinent reveal a unique tapestry woven from the natural patterns and pastel hues of primeval Africa and the more geometric, vivid shades and forms that modern man has imposed upon the scene. In southern Africa, perhaps alone on the 'Dark Continent', modern technology has achieved a symbiosis with the rhythms of an older dynasty. Highways stretch like aluminium strips past rural settlements that have otherwise changed little over thousands of years; the shadows cast by modern cities lose form and intensity as they disappear into the mysterious bushveld, or sink into the depths of the oceans.

The landscapes of southern Africa are interlinked like pieces of a giant jigsaw puzzle: the base is made up of geological units that date from over three billion years ago, to those deposited over the past ten thousand years. The picture superimposed upon the base comprises the natural fauna and flora of each region, fading and mingling with those around it, and cities, farms and pastoral scenes. While each image meshes subtly with the next, this subcontinent harbours one of the greatest contrasts of natural regions on earth.

This contrast ranges from the ancient deserts of the Namibian coastline to tropical forests on the Zululand and Maputoland coast; burning valleys with names like 'Hell' are wedged between crinkled sandstone crags of the Cape mountains; the lofty spires and towering walls of the Drakensberg rise from the rolling green farmlands of the Natal and Transkei Midlands; forested escarpment walls drop 300 metres to the eastern Transvaal Lowveld – the Bushveld of old Africa that stretches to the north, into Zimbabwe and Botswana beyond.

Left: *In winter, snow often dusts the Mostertshoek peaks, seen here from the Breede River.*

Namibia

Previous pages: *The largest sand dunes in the world encircle the open pan of Sossusvlei, in the heart of the Namib Desert. The source of the Namib's sand is a submarine delta formed off the mouth of the Orange River. Topsoil stripped from the interior colours the river and is deposited on the western continental shelf. Wind-driven inshore currents then carry the sand northwards and deposit it along the southern Namibian coastline. From here the grains are pushed ever northwards, eventually to be trapped in the Kuiseb River Canyon and returned to the sea when the river comes down in flood.*

Above: *No water flows between the Cunene River, which marks Namibia's north-western border, and the Orange River which marks the southern border. The Cunene River rises in the rain-soaked hills of southern Angola and then passes through the Kaokoveld – Namibia's most forsaken territory.*

Right: *Along its course to the cold Atlantic Ocean, the Cunene River plunges into a narrow chasm of the Epupa Falls. Wild date palms line the river and gorge, but beyond that very little survives.*

If ever God created a land in a fit of anger, then it would appear that Namibia is that land. Jumbled rocky wastelands, forged by the earth's internal fires, give way to scorching desert dunes and gravel plains to the west and south, to the endless red dunes of the Kalahari Basin to the east and to insect-infested swamplands to the north. But after the first impression of barrenness and desolation, one begins to perceive a far richer, more subtle interplay of nature where unique forms have evolved, sometimes bizarre, sometimes grand, to complement the country's magnificence. To those people who have journeyed through Namibia's eternal landscapes, the country is a show-

case of delicate interactions between the land and its life forms.

The rugged north-western corner of Namibia, called the Kaokoveld, is as daunting as any part of the country. Here one perceives a land that is awesome and vast, its grandeur forged by terrible forces over aeons. The vistas seem to reach to infinity. Pale landscapes simply fade into the paleness of the over-arching sky, gnarled mountains and tortured trees stand starkly silhouetted against furious storm clouds that seem to be lighted from within.

Although the Marienfluss mountainland seems to consist of only pale wind-scattered sands trapped between the convoluted strata of

Above: *Namibia is a geologist's paradise. Surreal rockscapes stretch from horizon to horizon, bare of all but the sparsest vegetation. Not only are they clearly visible, but the rocks here are particularly interesting, being mostly of volcanic origin and shot through with veins of many precious and economically valuable crystals and minerals. This rounded granite pavement in the Skeleton Coast National Park, crissed-crossed by quarzitic veins, is part of the Old Granite Suite which is widespread in southern Africa.*

dark volcanic rock, small herds of Hartmann's zebra can sometimes be seen cantering across the burning sands, as they search for scant pastures in the surrounding hills. It is also inhabited by the ova-Himba people, who represent probably the most primitive culture remaining intact in southern Africa, now that the last of the Kalahari Bushmen have given up their purely hunter-gatherer existence. The severe Kaokoveld demands that man and beast living there must exist as nomads, wandering from waterhole to intermittent spring, with only the Cunene River on the extreme north-western border offering the security of permanent water.

The entire western coastline of Namibia is covered by the sands of the world's oldest unchanged desert, the Namib, where hot easterly winds blow stinging plumes of sand off the dune crests and into the frothy, chilling Atlantic surf. The stark contrast between land and sea is the essence of the hostile Skeleton Coast where forlorn carcasses of seals and whales, of wrecked ships and sailors lie scattered on the beaches, trapped by time.

Here nature offers no respite for the weak, for they fall prey to

Above: *The Afrikaans name for the genus* Commiphora *is 'kanniedood', or 'cannot die' – and it is not difficult to see why. This commiphora growing in the bleak Kaokoveld is not dead, but being deciduous, has dropped its leaves. In a land where vegetation is scarce, most parts of the tree are used for medicinal or other purposes. Bushmen make arrow poison from these trees, and larva of the beetle* Diamphidia *feed exclusively on them.*

jackals and brown hyaenas which prowl the beaches. These scavengers skulk through seal rookeries to kill the weak and dying, eat discarded placentas, or to find anything edible which the sea has cast out onto the sand. The desiccating wind is just as merciless, its moan more mocking than the howl of predators.

Near the southern edge of the Namib Naukluft Park the Tsauchab River flows through limestone formations at Sesriem Canyon and then dissipates into the clay bowl at Sossusvlei. Surrounding the pan are the highest sand dunes in the world, their slopes performing arabesques in form and colour as shadows and hues shift throughout the day, their serpentine crests twisting like the motion of desert adders.

The first diamonds found in Namibia date back to 1908, when a railway labourer working on a new line between Lüderitz and Keetmanshoop recognized the gems gleaming in the shifting desert sands about 200 kilometres south of Sossusvlei. A diamond rush over the next 20 years saw the establishment of towns at Elizabeth Bay, Pomona and Kolmanskop, complete with skittle alleys, theatres

Previous pages: *For months and even years Etosha lies dusty and forlorn, its white soda crust baking and cracking in the sun. Then when summer storms do come, the 'great white pan' fills up, fed by a network of channels that radiate out across the arid savanna flatness.*

Above: *Antarctic middle water wells up along the south-west African coastline, creating an icy sea that starves the land of rain. But with the icy water comes a 'soup' of nutrients, hauled up to within the sun's penetrating influence. These minerals and organic particles form the basis of a food-web that includes the world's richest pelagic fish reserves. Cape fur seals rest and breed on the bleak Namib coast, living 'off the fat of the sea'.*

Right: *Flamingoes utilize the shallow, brackish waters of coastal pans, estuaries and inlets along the Namibian coast. Etosha Pan is their most important breeding site on the subcontinent, but they are nomads and wander from place to place as food supplies dictate. The shallows of Lüderitz Bay and Sandwich Harbour are favourite feeding grounds.*

and swimming baths, ice machines, the clang of shovels on rock and the grind of machinery.

German fashions from the early 20th-century can still be seen in the architecture at Kolmanskop, where sand now covers the streets and spills into the hallways. Where formerly crowds thronged to find the bread and cakes still hot and fresh, now only the eerie wind knocks at the door that announces *Bäckerei*. The window-rims of the bakery contain shards of shattered glass, frosted by the driven sand, and its doors creak on rusted hinges.

The new diamond industry caused Lüderitz Bay to become a thriving port – distinguished visitors were received from afar, delicate garden seedlings arrived from Europe, the latest international fashions and the best technology were available. But the diamonds at Kolmanskop were soon all gathered up and the diamond rush shifted south to Oranjemund, which remains the centre of the diamond industry today.

Lüderitz declined, but was temporarily revived as an important fishing port in the early 1960s. Within 20 years, however, ignorance and greed brought about the collapse of what were potentially the world's richest fishing grounds. Now, once again, Lüderitz languishes in isolation on the edge of the Namib Desert.

Nearly half the surface of Namibia is covered by rocks of the Nama and Damara geological groups, which have been sculpted by rivers and weathering into surreal landscapes, where erosion has revealed the sinuous banding of pale, pastel-coloured metamorphic rocks and darker volcanic strata. The Fish River Canyon – the most impressive natural spectacle in the country and the second deepest and most extensive canyon in the world – has been cut into horizontal layers of the Nama group of rocks. The sheer chasms and interlocking spurs draw the eye down to the floor of the canyon, where the tool of its creation, the Fish River, twists like a hungry serpent through the convoluted gorges.

The canyon is an example of the country's gigantic proportions and its immense emptiness. Only when the rays of the dawn and the evening sun slip through the buttresses and over the canyon's lip to wash its massive walls in muted light can the range of colours be appreciated: tiers of pale grey limestone, yellow, greenish and blue micaceous shale and soft pink, red or purple sandstone are interbedded with hard, black dolerite and reddish-brown quartzite. The ripple marks on many of these layers hint at their watery origins. Two layers of glacial deposits are evidence of the incredible climatic range that prevailed during the time in which these deposits were laid down – from deep sea, through shallow marine and possibly deltaic and swamp conditions, to ice-locked expanses and finally to wind-scoured desert.

Etosha, a great white pan in the north, is an extraordinary natu-

ral phenomenon that is thought to have once been part of a great lake that stretched from here to the Okavango Delta and the Makgadikgadi Salt Pans beyond. For most of the year the pan lies dormant, a salt-encrusted bowl with no outlet. Ground squirrels and suricates stand at their burrow entrances, sniffing the still atmosphere, always alert; nothing moves on the blinding, silence-engulfed surface of the pan. Then spring breezes awaken and cumulo-nimbus clouds swell in the thermals above the pan. By the end of November the clouds are bruised purple with their heavy loads of water; lightning whips, thunder cracks and a sudden rush of cool wind announces the summer rains.

As soon as the network of pans and the frill of watercourses are inundated, giraffes, gemsbok and springbok, elephant and lions and herds of zebra and wildebeest appear from every point on the plains beyond, which are part of the subcontinent's largest game reserve. The most spectacular entrance is made by the pink clouds of flamingoes that arrive to feed on the salty algal 'soup' that rejuvenates Eto-

Above: *Although the rivers in Namibia seldom flow, canyons such as this one on the Skeleton Coast's Uniab River hold water in all but the driest years. Animals learn where to look for water, and these linear oases through the desert sustain animals as large as elephants – each one of which requires about 200 litres of drinking water a day.*

sha. The pan is the most important breeding place in southern Africa for lesser flamingoes. Greater flamingoes also breed here, in smaller numbers. These similar species are able to live side by side by having different food requirements: the lesser species filters the top layer of the water for its tiny algal plankton, while the greater flamingoes stir up the mud for small crustaceans and other invertebrates.

The lesser flamingoes lay single eggs in volcano-shaped mud nests which are found in dense colonies on the pan's mud flats. After incubating for one moon's cycle, fluffy charcoal-coloured chicks emerge and are fed on regurgitated algal 'soup'. As the waters of the pan begin to evaporate under the sun's fierce onslaught, the chicks must toddle after the receding shoreline, while their parents continue to feed them. Many chicks cannot survive the arduous trek of up to 80 kilometres, which ends only when the final mud pool vanishes and they are ready for flight, to begin life as Africa's most glamorous nomads.

Spreading out to the north of Etosha are the seasonal swamplands of Ovamboland, a giant floodplain that is home to nearly half Namibia's population. A shifting labyrinth of watercourses, called oshanas, drains Ovamboland's annual floods. They are fringed with tall *Hyphaene* palm trees, the fruits of which are eaten or used to make a traditional fermented beer, while the fronds are used to make mats and baskets. Most of the region's former woodlands have all been cleared to make way for fields and villages, giving Ovamboland its distinctive look. But this uncontrolled exploitation may ultimately cause it to become a wasteland.

To the east of Ovamboland lies Kavango and the narrow strip of Caprivi, which reaches like an outstretched hand past Angola, Botswana and Zambia to touch the north-western tip of Zimbabwe. The seasonal floodplains continue right through Kavango province and to the 'wrist' of the Caprivi Strip. Here the Caprivi broadens out into a hand shape, defined by the Mashi, Linyanti, Chobe and Zambezi rivers. Seasonal pans and swamps are replaced by large lakes and inland deltas, like Liambezi Lake and the Linyanti Delta.

This north-eastern strip of land is only sparsely populated by humans, but continued military presence here over the past 20 years has had a profound impact on the wildlife and its wilderness character. Nonetheless, it is wild, wonderful bushveld, where men paddle dugouts across the waterways; small villages shelter beneath giant kiaat, wild fig and mahogany trees; and hippos yawn in the deep blue pools. In the Caprivi the sun sets behind silhouetted baobabs and palm trees, casting glorious colour across the entire sky, while drumbeats fill the twilight, as if to placate the spirits of the night.

Above: Gazania krebsiana *grows throughout the south- and north-western Cape. This is one of the daisy species which contribute to the famed Namaqualand flower spectacle. They are annuals which germinate in response to early autumn rains and then grow throughout winter. With the first spring rains they quickly bloom, seed and then die as summer advances.*

Western Cape

Previous pages: *In the rugged mountains of the Boland, man has created a harmonious symbiosis with his environment. This is wine country, where vineyards flourish in the lee of the Groot Drakenstein mountains, and the white gables of Cape Dutch farmsteads echo the forms of the folded sandstone slabs.*

Below: *The south-western Cape's Mediterranean climate means long, hot summers and cold, wet winters – and nowhere is this more apparent than in the Cedarberg mountains. These extremes in weather are reflected in the broken rock landscape near the Wolfberg Arch. The Cedarberg Wilderness area is famed for its unique fynbos species and its weird rock formations, chiselled by the summer's fiery heat, and the contrasting icy winter temperatures.*

Right: *Bird Island in Lambert's Bay is the largest of six breeding islands of the Cape gannet, where these large marine birds breed in tightly-packed colonies. Their nests are made from piles of guano lined with sticks and seaweed.*

The western Cape is a spectacular corner of southern Africa where natural splendour seems to have been concentrated. Ranks of massive grey crags enclose white-fringed, cobalt-blue bays where, in spring, whales frolic in the shallows. Great arches of chalice-shaped proteas, tiny bell-like ericas and delicate orchids, gladioluses and a thousand other plants bloom abundantly on the mountain slopes. Exuberant streams have carved secret, gorges deep into the jagged ranges, plunging through trout-filled pools, and bursting out into fertile valleys where orchards stand in ripe rows. Grapes, too, do well in the dry, hot summers and cool, wet winters, and vineyards thread across the slopes.

The Cape Peninsula, dominated by the formidable ramparts of Table Mountain, is the epicentre of the region and is its social focus. The oldest city on the subcontinent rests within the semi-circular embrace of two flanking mountains – Devil's Peak and Lion's Head: Cape Town, the Mother City, the Tavern of the Seas, a city situated at 'the fairest cape in all the circumference of the earth', as Sir Francis Drake declared it to be. Cape Town retains its links with its colonial past: 17th-century slave quarters and military barracks are renovated as sought-after city residences; 18th-century townhouses have become restaurants or stylish offices; baroque and neo-classical public buildings still stand next to modern highrises.

The city recedes southwards along the western Atlantic seaboard, which weaves past cliffs and around coves that contain Mediterranean-style suburbs. Towards the storm-lashed headland of Cape Point, one passes long arcs of beach where surfers ride like torpedoes in the tubing breakers, and prolific birdlife decorates the estuarine wetlands, and fishing villages and hide-away retreats tucked into the hills. Moving to the south-east along the Peninsula's mountain spine, suburbs almost as old as the city itself nestle beside parkland, which in turn blends through pine woods to the delicious freshness of Newlands Forest, complete with moss- and fern-frilled cascades and arcades of giant afro-montane trees, adjoining the visual extravaganza of the National Botanic Garden at Kirstenbosch.

Beyond the historic vineyards on the slopes of the Constantia-berg is the magnificent sweep of False Bay, with its focus at festive Muizenberg. Brightly painted changing boxes at the famous beach at St James precede the colourful bustle of Kalk Bay's quaint fishing harbour. City dazzle and seaboard odours, salt-encrusted old boats bobbing at their moorings, centuries-old homesteads and modern housing estates, rustic charm in the valleys and fynbos wilderness in the mountains – past and future, nature and technology seem to intersect at this far-flung corner of Africa. For scenic diversity few places in the world can compare with the Cape Peninsula, with its contrasts of natural areas, the dramatic mountain and sea panoramas, the never-ending parade of vignettes of European and African culture, and noisy harbour scenes.

Beyond the spreading metropolis of Greater Cape Town lie the Boland winelands to the east; picturesque old towns with their clean, white Cape Dutch architecture hide within the folds of gargantuan mountain ranges. A little way up the west coast, the Strand-veld's reticent beauty evokes images of past, unhurried lifestyles. In the fishing towns and villages of St Helena Bay, small trawlers wallow in the bay harbours, fishermen in bright sou'westers and woollen caps row their dinghies out through the morning surf. The apricot sun ripens on the liquid horizon, casting broad brush strokes of light on the water and tinting the breakers with a soft golden glint. The white cottages of the fisherfolk at Paternoster cling like barnacles

Above: *If he saw this today, would Sir Francis Drake still call it 'the fairest cape in all the circumference of the earth'; Would Jan van Riebeeck believe his eyes? When Van Riebeeck arrived in 1652 to colonize the 'Cape of Good Hope', wild animals and small bands of Hottentots were all that roamed these shores.*

Right above: *Plumes of cloud break over Table Mountain and the flanking Twelve Apostles. The south-east wind casts Table Mountain's famous 'cloth' as the moisture-laden air is forced over the mountain and condenses at that exact height.*

Right below: *Looking northwards along Chapman's Peak Drive to Hout Bay. The sinuous road was built on the interface between the underlying Cape Granite, which forms domed masses and rounded boulders, and the wafered cliffs of sandstone and shale.*

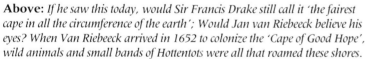

to the rocks that encircle the small bay. Upturned boats lie in the veld above the beach and daisies and gazanias poke their gay faces through holes in the peeling hulls.

Langebaan Lagoon, which lies just south of St Helena Bay, is one of the ecological wonders of southern Africa. Every spring more than 50 000 Palaearctic migrant birds travel from the ice-bound extremes of northern Europe and Greenland to feed on the salt marshes and

mud flats at the southern curve of the long, narrow inlet. The curlews with their long, curved beaks probe for crabs and prawns; greater flamingoes rake the mud for tiny invertebrate animals; greenshanks, elegant stilts and avocets sweep the water with their odd, upturned bills; turnstones, as their name implies, turn stones over with their beaks to reveal the small mud-dwellers on which they feed; sand-pipers patter about rapidly, feeding on worms and crabs, small molluscs and crustaceans; terns wheel in the air on scimitar wings as they hunt for fingerlings in the water beneath; pelicans form nets with their beaks which sweep through the deeper water for fish ... at Langebaan Lagoon there is enough for all.

More than two thirds of all the seasonally migrating waders which visit Langebaan are curlew sandpipers, small birds with mottled grey-brown plumage, a hunched posture and long, down-curved beaks. Individual flocks which may comprise as many as 2 000 birds, settle on exposed mud banks to fatten up before departing for their breeding grounds in far Siberia.

Left: *The Rooiels River, which flows into False Bay, is named after the red alder trees which grow in the verdant gorge. These large forest trees can be identified by the 'butter spoon' stipules which enclose the buds at the branch tips. Sunset silhouettes Devils's Peak, Table Mountain and the Peninsula mountains across the bay.*

Below: *The sheared-off bases of sandstone folds plunge into the sea along False Bay's western shore. When the Cape mountains were folded, up to 200 million years ago, it is believed that these mountains encircled the entire bay. Some peaks soared as high as 6 000 metres – but erosion has since made beach sand out of them. The original Table Mountain sandstones were, incidentally, deposited as beach and shallow marine sands from about 350 to 300 million years ago.*

Despite its name, Langebaan Lagoon is not a lagoon, neither is it an estuary; it is a very long and narrow inlet that was formed by successive rises and falls in sea level over millions of years, where a gap in the surrounding granite hillocks allowed the fluctuating ocean to erode a narrow passage into the land. The answer to the seeming mystery as to why the water in this narrow inlet is so clear, when the sea outside is a thick soup of plankton and suspended particles, is to be found on the sea floor at the mouth of the inlet. Here, filter-feeding white mussels (*Donax serra*) live in such a tightly packed colony that they filter out most of the particles in the water as the tide flows through the mouth, leaving it as clear as the water around coral reefs, yet with the same salinity level as the sea.

Opposite the mouth of Langebaan, the heavily industrialized port of Saldanha Bay contrasts sharply with the serenity of the inlet. To allow for the loading of iron ore onto large ships, a causeway was built from the mainland to Skaap Island, one of a number of islands that lie at the mouth of Langebaan Lagoon, and which are important

Above: *When the Protestant Huguenots arrived at the Cape between 1688 and 1690, the Dutch colonists had already established vineyards on the slopes of Constantiaberg, outside Cape Town. The arrival of these French farmers, however, did much to influence the character of the European community, and to improve the quality of its wines.*

Right: *In 1988 the tri-centennial of the arrival of the French Huguenots was celebrated in Franschhoek, the beautiful corner of the Berg River valley in which they settled. Today there are 12 farms in the valley which make up the 'Vignerons de Franschhoek'. This wine-makers' association markets the valley's produce, mainly Chardonnay, Chenin Blanc, Sauvignon Blanc and other French-style white wines.*

Pages 34-35: *A scarlet* kniphofia *(red hot poker) brightens the dull bracken and fynbos veld in the foothills of the Langkloof mountains. When not in flower, the fynbos appears lifeless and monotonous. However, in spring, the proteas, ericas, orchids, watsonias and a thousand other flowering plants set the veld ablaze with colour.*

breeding colonies for many species of marine birds. In fact, Malgas, Jutten and Skaap islands are home to breeding colonies of most of the remaining black oystercatchers in the world and a third of all the southern sub-species of swift tern, as well as jackass penguins, Cape and bank cormorants, kelp gulls, caspian terns and other species.

The traditional settlements at Kraalbaai and Churchhaven depict remnants of the 'old ways', where the fishing communities with their fish 'kraals' in the bay have recently been incorporated into the newly proclaimed Langebaan National Park. In the development of this reserve, designated to protect what has been referred to as 'the jewel of the west coast', the terms of reference of the National Parks Board were extended to allow for the protection of traditional human settlements and activities that are harmonious and consistent with the surrounding natural landscape.

Inland, across the wheatlands of the Swartland, the land sweeps up in impressive parabolic curves to the Grootwinterhoek and Cedarberg mountain ranges. During the summer, these mountains blister in the dry Mediterranean heat, while in winter they are lashed by rain and covered with rock-shattering snow and ice. These rugged ridges, peaceful valleys, remote plateaux and isolated peaks encapsulate a wilderness to rival the Drakensberg's grandeur and the floral wonders of the Hottentots-Holland mountains.

The Cedarberg is named for the forests of Clanwilliam cedar trees that were all but exterminated two centuries ago for their fine timber. Today the range is known among mountaineers for its remoteness and grand scale, and for its many fantastical rock formations, sculpted by extreme weather and mechanical erosion. The 20-metre-high Maltese Cross stands on a clinkered plain below Sneeukop, the highest peak in the Cedarberg; Tafelberg and The Spout rise from the elevated, natural walkway of Die Trap; south of here stands the Raadsaal, which looks as if it came from the pages of the Brothers Grimm's fairy tales. The Wolfberg Cracks tower over the settlement of Dwarsrivier, while the spectacular Wolfberg Arch beyond looks down onto the parched scrubland of the Tanqua Karoo. On the highest and most exposed peaks grows the lovely, white puff-ball snow protea.

Tucked into the valley of the Tra-tra River, almost out of sight

Above: *The southern Cape coast at Waenhuiskrans, near the historical fishing village of Arniston, is typically composed of calcareous cliffs which represent a previous sea level. The sea's relentless wave action has eroded many caves into the cliffs, such as the 'waenhuis' (wagon house) here and 'De Kelders' (the cellars) nearer to Hermanus.*

Left: *On the mountains above the Bot River near Hermanus, are found some of the most interesting and rare species of flowering plants in the entire Cape Floral Kingdom.*

Right: *De Hoop Nature Reserve is a controversial one, for the Defence Force uses part of it as a missile testing range, and the observation towers are sited on the Potberg, home of the only remaining breeding colony of Cape vultures in the province. The reserve protects a rich diversity of natural habitats which are fast disappearing under cultivation of the surrounding southern Cape wheatlands.*

below the Wolfberg Arch, the village of Wuppertal hides like a Shangri-la. To get there, one must negotiate the serpentine Pakhuis Pass and travel down into the Bidouw Valley, where the rubble beside the road reveals fossils of shellfish that lived over 200 million years ago when the shales of the Bokkeveld were deposited along a long-vanished coastal margin. In springtime, this valley is transformed for a few weeks into a kaleidoscopic blaze of flowering annuals.

The historic winelands terminate in the north in the shadow of Grootwinterhoek Peak, around the town of Tulbagh, named in honour of the 18th-century governor, Ryk Tulbagh. It lies in the long valley between the Grootwinterhoek, the Hexrivier and the Witsenberg mountain ranges, where the Berg River has cut its way out of the western Cape's mountain vortex. From here to Stellenbosch, the winelands follow the curve of the Cape's folded ranges, painting the

valleys green in spring, russet and gold in autumn. In February the vines droop with bunches of taut, sweet, pale-green hanepoot, riesling and steen grapes, or glow with splashes of deep purple – tart cabernet, cinsaut and pinot noir grapes. The curvilinear gables of the stately Cape Dutch homesteads which characterize the winelands echo the shapes of the rock buttresses which stand as dramatic backdrops to the estates, stark white moulding accentuated by the mute grey sentinels.

The headwaters of the western Cape's principal waterway, the Breede River, rise on the gnarled slopes of the Hexrivier and Witsenberg mountains, carving their way through the enclave of Ceres and the wide valley wherein Worcester stands, forcing their way between the Riviersonderend mountains and the Langeberg, from Robertson to Swellendam, before wearily emerging on the wide coastal plain that stretches to Agulhas – the southern tip of Africa. At Malgas a pont ferries cars and people across the broad, lethargic river, where trees and a lonely cottage are reflected in the dappled waters. The

Below: *An idyllic scene in the Langkloof mountains; although these pine trees lend an alpine atmosphere to the landscape, they are in fact alien trees which invade the natural mountain vegetation. Once established, they are hard to eradicate and, if left unchecked, will keep spreading, and eventually replace the natural flora.*

Breede River breaches land at Infanta in St Sebastian Bay, where, in spring, southern right whales come to nurse their calves. These leviathans play in the calm waters of the southern Cape coast's bays, leaping out of the water and smashing down again, their enormous flukes slapping the sea.

The wide coastal plain between Swellendam and Cape Agulhas is covered with fertile shale-derived soils and limestone, which give rise to quite different natural vegetation. The shales once supported dense expanses of coastal fynbos, but there is very little left of this flora. It has made way for wheat fields that cover the land like a corduroy patchwork between Caledon and Riversdale. The limestone surface to the south of Bredasdorp hails from the mid-Cretaceous and Tertiary periods (about 50 million and less than 20 million years ago respectively) when the sea advanced and retreated across the wave-cut plain, depositing shells which decomposed to form calcium-rich soil.

Over the last few hundreds of millions of years the Cape Super-group of rocks, which forms the region's mountain ranges, was buckled and twisted during the movements of continental plates. At one stage the highest peaks stood over six kilometres above sea level, and they have since been eroded until only their bases, composed of Table Mountain Sandstone, still show, like the worn-down stumps of the teeth of an ancient creature. The Bokkeveld shales were deposited on top of the sandstones, but they are softer and so have been completely eroded away from the the upthrust folds and remain only in the valleys, with layers of sandstone beneath them where the folds dip below the surface. The creatures on earth experience great trauma whenever the surface of the planet erupts with volcanoes or sections of mountains crumble through erosion and the constant force of gravity. But the semi-solid surface is only a tiny fraction of the earth's mass, and geomorphological activity, of what seems to us to be calamatous proportions, is really just a fine sandpapering of the planet's surface, to ensure that it spins evenly on its axis as it spirals through the cosmos.

Above: *A painted lady (*Gladiolus debilis*) shows its coquettish face. Flowers such as this, the 'moederkappie', marsh rose, and blushing bride are much-prized jewels in the Cape's floral heritage.*

The Garden Route and Little Karoo

Previous pages: *The Keurbooms River meets the Indian Ocean in Plettenberg Bay, where the Tsitsikamma mountains peer over the Garden Route coastal plain. This area is the interface between the temperate fynbos, and the subtropical climatic and vegetational zones. Magnificent beaches, extensive yellowwood forests, rugged mountains and kind weather make this the most coveted stretch for recreation along the entire southern African coast.*

Southern Africa is without doubt the most variable region of its size in the world, so that the word 'contrast' features regularly in descriptions of it. However, this description is seldom given to the mountainous, coastal country between George and Humansdorp, along the south-eastern edge of the subcontinent, and yet it has perhaps the greatest natural contrasts in so confined an area. Temperate evergreen forests cloak the shady southern slopes of the mountain ranges, well watered by coastal mists and year-round rainfall, while succulent desert plants cling to the blistered northern valley floors, sweltering in the rain shadow of the mountains.

Driving along the Garden Route highway which skirts the Wilderness Lakes, a grand panorama alternatively opens out or recedes as the road winds through the coastal hills, through the precipitous

Left: *A fine display of* Ruschia *species (family Mesembryanthemaceae) near Touws River in the Karoo.*

Above: *Ostrich farming has long been one of the main commercial enterprises of the Little Karoo valleys. Ostriches are not naturally found in this area, but the southern African sub-species (*Struthio camelus australis*) has been interbred in the Little Karoo with the northern sub-species (*S. c. syriacus*), to improve the feathers for commercial trade.*

storm clouds that fill up an afternoon sky. Bank upon bank of blue, grey and dark green humps catch the sun's rays in slivers along their eastern ridges. As the mist lifts the lakes are dappled with light and shadow, giving off the sheen of mercury when the soft light breaks over the hills, while later, in the afternoon glare, their surfaces reflect like irregular aluminium offcuts tossed haphazardly among the foothills.

These lakes are really a series of estuarine lagoons, as they are fed by numerous streams which rise in the mountains and which have been blocked by a previous drop in sea level, leaving their mouths high and dry. Swartvlei still a has limited outlet to the sea at Sedgefield Beach, resulting in some tidal interaction. All these lakes are experiencing a natural cycle of siltation that will eventually turn them into shallow, algae-covered vleis, then marshy reed-beds, until finally they will disappear altogether. This is the natural cycle of all lakes, but at the estuary at Wilderness (and almost all the estuaries along the South African coast) the process has been greatly accelerated by erosion, which is the result of bad farming practices; by the damming of rivers and tapping off of water, which reduces river flow into the estuaries and reduces their self-clearing capabilties; and by pollution, which either kills off the filter-functioning plants or causes them to proliferate and die off quickly, thereby adding significantly to the bottom silt each year.

From Nature's Valley to the Grootrivier mouth near Humansdorp, the Tsitsikamma Coastal National Park straddles the most magnificent coastal scenery of southern Africa. Most of this 67-kilometre-long stretch is a rocky coastline, with high cliffs cut

Kaaimans River Gorge, skirting the 'lake district' between Wilderness and Sedgefield, until it emerges into the broad valley flooded by the Knysna Lagoon, which is, strictly speaking, not a lagoon but an estuary. The Wilderness Lakes lie on a former marine terrace, trapped between high, vegetated, coastal dunes and the wooded foothills of the Cape Fold mountains.

In the mornings a soft mist hangs upon the surface of Langvlei, obscuring in a silky veil the iron bridge that carries the narrow-guage Apple Express over the Serpentine. Bird calls rise through the fog on Rondevlei, and the fog condenses on the metal-cool surface of Swartvlei, whose jagged arms embrace the surrounding foothills. Waterfowl potter along the reed fringe of Groenvlei. Looking northwards, the Outeniqua mountains loom across the wide horizon like

Above: *The Dwyka River cuts through the mighty Swartberg range near Calitzdorp. The valleys that lie in the rain shadow of the Cape Fold mountains form the Little Karoo region. These semi-desert fingers are an inland extension of the Succulent Karoo vegetation zone that lies along the Cape west coast, north of Elands Bay.*

Right: *Winter's cold fronts dust the Swartberg with snow. These mountains form a great barrier between the Little Karoo and Great Karoo. In summer they are scorched and desiccated by the African sun, while in winter they intercept blizzards that sweep across the Cape from the Southern Ocean.*

through by deep gorges. An angry, restless sea pounds the shore, but the rocky beaches are a kaleidoscope of inter-tidal life. The Tsitsi-kamma coastline is the meeting place of temperate and sub-tropical marine environments, so an interesting mix of species occurs along this wild coastal margin.

Massed beds of brown mussels and limpets cling to the wave-pounded shore. Limpets may number up to 2 500 individuals in a square metre of rocky beach. Bright waving stalks of jelly-like ane-mones, clusters of spiky sea-urchins, rubbery carpets of zoanthids and colourful, flowery algal fronds infest the more sheltered rock pools. But all is not peaceful in these pools, where whelks and star-fish are aggressive predators of the other creatures. Nothing here is harmful to man, though – not even the octopuses whose powerful beaks could inflict a painful bite if ever they were used for this pur-pose. Only by seeing the vibrancy and abundance of this protected coastline can we appreciate the damage done to coasts by modern man, who wantonly collects various organisms for bait and then over-fishes the waters, who strips the rocks for mussels and oysters, and who so casually dumps his domestic and industrial wastes into the sea.

The popular Otter Trail winds along the ruggedly beautiful coastline of the park, where Cape clawless otters hunt in the shal-

lows for crabs, though hikers seldom spot them, where dusky dol-
phins tear through the swells, Cape fur seals dart after fish like torpedoes and loll on the surface to bask, and southern right whales come
to calve in the nearby bays. Observant hikers may identify many of
the 35 species of marine birds found here, including black oystercatchers, sooty shearwaters, Arctic skuas and various terns and gulls.
High yellowwood forest occupies deeper valleys, shady slopes and
all the higher ground between sea and mountain tops, while low
scrub forest grows in more exposed places where the soil is fertile.

On exposed, less fertile slopes, coastal fynbos blazes with erica
and mimetes inflorescences, conebushes, pincushions, sugarbushes
and other proteas, interspersed with scarlet Knysna lilies, butter-yel-
low gazanias and the compact, fiery, orange-red blooms of krantz
aloes that grow on rocky outcrops overlooking the sea. The nectar
from these flowers attracts malachite, orange-breasted and collared
sunbirds, with their dazzling metallic plumages, while grysbok and
grey duiker, three species of mongoose, baboons and dassies (rock
hyraxes) inhabit the fynbos and scrub forest.

The tall, humid podocarpus forest, for which the Garden Route is
most admired, takes its name from the towering yellowwood trees
(*Podocarpus falcatus* and *P. latifolius*) that characterize them. Their large

Left: *Lookout Beach at Plettenberg Bay. During the summer vacation this coastal resort changes from a sleepy town of about 8 000 permanent residents to a seething throng of over 60 000 holiday-makers.*

Below: *Looking westward along the Tsitsikamma coastline towards Plettenberg Bay, the Tsitsikamma Coastal National Park offers refuge from the madding crowds. Here shy otters play along the wild and rocky shore, and nature lovers can hike in relative isolation.*

Above: *The serene waters of Swartvlei, the largest of the Wilderness Lakes, and the only one still open to the sea.*

clusters of small, bright green leaves hang festooned with pale green streamers of the lichen called 'old man's beard'. There are also the creamy-white flowering sprays of forest nuxia trees, stinkwoods and wild olives, white and red alders, saffronwood, Cape beech and holly trees, wild peach and pear – a spectacular variety. The trees and cliffs are draped with mosses and ferns, of which there are 25 different species, and lilies and orchids decorate the damp ground. Blue duiker and bushbuck, tree hyraxes and leopards still haunt the sombre labyrinths of these fecund woods.

The Tsitsikamma Forest is really made up of many large and small patches, relicts of the temperate evergreen forests that once covered a large part of south-eastern Africa. But over the past few thousand years the climate here has become gradually and steadily drier, so that these once-great forests have shrunk to a size where they are hardly viable as a healthily functioning biome. During the past two centuries man has helped reduce the stature of the remaining forests by burning and cutting them. When the protective margin is disturbed, or roads are cut through a forest, a wound is opened that allows weeds, fire, excessive light and dryness to damage the cool and

Above: *It is obvious why 'Eilandvlei' is so named. Although the Wilderness Lakes are considered to be a high priority conservation area under the control of the National Parks Board, holiday and recreation use is graded in zones along these lagoons. Eilandvlei is zoned as a 'high use' area, where private holiday homes have been built on the naturally stabilized fossil dunes.*

Left: *The western verge of the Knysna Heads, through which the Knysna River finds the sea. No sand bars or dunes block the river mouth, and very little erosion occurs in the short catchment area to silt up the estuary. Consequently, the mouth is deep and allows the estuary to be continually scoured by strong tidal action.*

moist microclimate. With active protection it may be possible to save what temperate forests still remain, but as long as mankind continues to expand his domain they are unlikely ever again to spread outwards.

The Outeniqua and Tsitsikamma mountains lie clothed in fynbos and forest, like close folds of velvet and corduroy. This lush vegetation benefits from the generous year-round rain which is intercepted on the southern, sea-facing slopes of the mountains. But behind these ranges the long, dry, interleading valleys receive generally less than 200 millimetres of rain a year. These valleys make up the Little Karoo region, which is a rain shadow desert smothered by the bunched-up pleats of rock. While the geology of the Little Karoo (which lies inland of and parallel to the Garden Route, mainly between the Outeniqua and Swartberg ranges) is similar to that of the Cape Fold mountains, the vegetation is a south-eastward extension of the arid Succulent Karoo Biome. This biological unit is found mainly along the Cape west coast, in the south abutting the Fynbos Biome's Strandveld component from about Verlorenvlei, to the Orange River, where it blends into the bleak Namib Desert.

Above: *Through the heart of the Tsitsikamma forest reserve, the Bloukrans River has cut this impressive gorge. This picture shows clearly the marine-cut terrace, representing a previous sea level.*

Although the Little Karoo is generally much drier and less fertile than the main Karoo, the many rivers that flow through these valleys allow for cultivation along narrow alluvial margins. Fruit orchids and even vineyards are found around Oudtshoorn and all along the Olifants River, which lies in the widest and longest valley of the Little Karoo.

More daunting are places like 'Die Hel' which lies in the long-forgotten Gamka River Valley, between the Swartberg and Seweweekspoort passes in the Groot Swartberg range. Spiky aloes and fleshy euphorbias grow on the rocky valley floor, while dry scrub and thorn bush clings to the jagged mountain slopes.

A small group of white herders chanced upon this remote valley in the early 19th-century, while searching for new grazing lands, and there they stayed. They lived in the old 'boer' tradition in the Gamka River Valley, forgotten by the outside world, until one generation ago when a road was cut through the valley and later a small school was built there. Dominating this part of the mighty Swartberg mountains, the Toverkop's twin bastions (2 126 metres), loom behind the town of Ladismith.

The Outeniqua and Swartberg mountains, Kammanassie and Baviaanskloof ranges, as well as the many smaller folded mountain ranges follow the coast line from Cape Town to Cape St Francis, almost 700 kilometres to the east. These mountains were all formed many millions of years ago when the enormous southern continent of Gondwanaland broke up into various plates. These movements of the earth's skin (which seems to us to be so solid, but is really like brittle plastic) resulted in a process called orographic folding: when the various plates that comprise the earth's crust push up against one another, one plate is invariably forced underneath another, and their edges either buckle upwards, or crumple in a series of folds.

Most of the world's highest mountain ranges have been formed in this way, including the Rockies and the Andes, the Alps and the Himalayas. In the case of the Cape's mountains, lateral folding coincided with compacting, so that today its peaks and ridges can be seen to be twisted and buckled both along and across the main axis of folding – which is from west to east. Before successive erosion cycles were set into motion, grinding down all protruding areas on the subcontinent and reducing mountains to beach sand, the peaks of the Cape Fold mountains would have been eclipsed only by the Himalayas and the highest peaks of the Andes. This gives us some idea as to how much older the mountains of southern Africa are than the others mentioned here, which will themselves one day be reduced to sea sand.

Above: Indigofera brachystachya *flowers splash the Tsitsikamma Coastal National Park with patches of mauve. Fire is an important controlling mechanism in this area, favouring the fynbos and damaging the forest – to which the burned-out trunks of young trees and flowering fynbos testify.*

The Great Karoo and Namaqualand

Previous pages: *From the summit of the Nuweveldberg in the Karoo National Park, one looks out over the Great Karoo 'vlaktes', and the Swartberg mountains in the far distance. Also visible to the informed visitor are the geological surfaces of the higher Gondwana surface, from before Gondwanaland broke up, and the lower African surface, eroded away since the breakup of this former composite southern landmass.*

Above: *In spring,* Ursinia *blooms beautify the cracked face of Namaqualand. The extent to which these annuals bloom each year depends on the amount of seasonal rain over the past few years. Being a dry area, it is unusual to have a widespread outburst as lovely as this more than once or twice in a decade.*

The Voortrekkers who ambled across the Karoo's open plains, between those typically flat-topped koppies, did not realize that they were passing through one of the earth's greatest natural wonders. Few of today's hasty travellers who speed across the seemingly monotonous interior, are aware of this either. But to travel through the Karoo can be like taking a journey through time, as if one were flipping through the early volumes of an encyclopaedia called 'Life on Earth', without really understanding the text. The language here is palaeontology and the letters are the bones of creatures that lie fossilized in the alternating layers of purple and blue-green mudstones, and creamy-yellow sandstones of the Karoo Supergroup of rocks, which covers about two-thirds of South Africa.

Some 280 million years ago South Africa was emerging from the grip of the great Permian ice age. As the ice-sheets retreated the climate became more temperate and the central portion of South Africa was revealed as a low-lying basin. A vast shallow sea covered the greater portion of southern Africa, extending onto the South American continent, at that time positioned along the west coast of Africa as part of the great prehistoric southern land mass, Gondwanaland. *Mesosaurus*, a semi-aquatic reptile which possessed a multitude of needle-like teeth and attained a maximum length of 2 metres, frequented this habitat and probably fed on another inhabitant, the small crayfish-like invertebrate *Notocaris*.

Over the next 90 million years the Karoo basin was inundated with rivers and streams depositing mud and sand, creating a lush

marshland which was invaded and exploited by a completely different group of animals called the mammal-like reptiles. They were the
dominant land vertebrates of their time and included groups such as
the horny-beaked dicynodonts, the large lumbering dinocephalians,
the rapacious flesh-eating gorgonopsians and therocephalians, and
the highly advanced cynodonts. Evolving gradually over a period of
approximately 50 million years, they finally gave rise to the first
primitive mammals. Nowhere else on earth is this transition so well
documented as in the rocks of the Karoo and that is the reason why
this seemingly barren landscape has been hailed by scientists as one
of the great natural wonders of the world.

The Karoo period was brought to a dramatic close by the massive
volcanic outpourings of the Drakensberg lavas. This was a series of
eruptions that covered most of the Karoo Basin, as well as other
smaller, scattered areas right across the subcontinent. Only the
mighty Drakensberg and Maluti mountains remain of the basalts
that were spewed out across the land, and which have been steadily
eroded away since then. But it was the lavas that did not find their
way to the surface that eventually went on to give the Karoo its typical flat-topped koppies. Basalt that is formed on the surface is relatively soft rock and therefore easily erodable. But when lava is
squeezed between sub-surface layers of rock, it is compressed and
cools very much more slowly than basalt, resulting in the formation
of iron-hard dolerite.

The Karoo mudstones are usually soft and easily chiselled away

Above: *Namaqualand's flowering spectacle is a curious one, being caused
largely by degradation of the veld through overgrazing. Although the gorgeous
daisies and other annuals that make up each spring flower show would
naturally bloom each year, the profusion of flowers seen in this picture is an
attempt by the plants each year to re-establish the vegetation's natural state.*

Above: *The dolerite caps that form the Three Sisters, between Beaufort West and Victoria West, once formed a continuous sill of rock. This 'iron rock' remains where the softer Beaufort shales have been eroded away, but in time even they will disappear.*

Left: *The plains that stretch out between Middelburg and Graaff-Reinet beneath the Bamboesberg, go under the name 'The Plains of Camdeboo'. Barely a tree stands on them, and early explorers and Dutch farmers rather appropriately called these sun-scorched plains the 'Valley of Desolation'.*

by the agents of erosion, but where these forces hit upon hard dolerite sills, they leave behind flat-topped hills such as the Three Sisters near Beaufort West and Harrismith's Platberg. The correct name for these hills is 'mesas', and when the dolerite cap is eventually worn back to form a finger-like protrusion, it is called a 'butte', such as Spandaukop above Graaff-Reinet.

In 1685, Governor Simon van der Stel set out with an expedition from the Castle in Cape Town into the dry northern regions, in search of the fabled Copper mountains and the wealthy empire of Monamotapa. Between the Sandveld and Namaqualand, the expedition stopped over at a small cave with a nearby spring that was known to the Hottentots and Bushmen. This stopover had been used three years previously when Van der Stel first sent a smaller expedition off to search for the copper and gold that Africa promised to yield. Olaf Bergh had then carved his name into the cave wall, and so began a tradition of graffiti that included many later travellers and dignitaries who passed that way. Thus the cave acquired its name of the 'Heerenlogement', meaning 'gentleman's lodging'. Among the many names to be seen on the cave walls are that of the Swedish botanist Karl Thunberg (1724), the French explorer and naturalist François Le Vaillant (1783), the German botanist K. L. Zeyher (1829) and Andrew Geddes Bain (1854).

While Olaf Bergh's party returned home after one of its members was killed by a lion near the Piketberg, Van der Stel reached the jumble of copper-coloured granite domes near present-day Springbok. Although they sank three shafts, his party failed to retrieve any significant amount of copper ore, certainly not enough to compensate for the arduous journey over rugged land to Cape Town, the heat, lack of water and general hostility of the land. Nearly two centuries

Above: *The Karoo's Beaufort Group rocks were laid down as mud and silt in a basin that then covered most of southern Africa. Giant reptiles roamed the swampy ground, and there they died, to be preserved in the mud and fossilized to form shales. Erosion has revealed these fossils, which lie like the text in the pages of the Karoo geological encyclopaedia. Now the swamplands have become semi-desert, fit only to carry sheep.*

later, however, this area became the world's principal copper-producer, until the discovery of diamonds along the west coast in 1926 eclipsed the copper industry in the region.

On a detour to the coast, Van der Stel crested a band of granite hills to look down into the hazy plain of the Buffalo River Valley. 'What a spectacle', he is recorded as having remarked, and today travellers to Port Nolloth and Alexander Bay still go by way of the impressive Spektakel Pass. The way is marked by outcrops of kokerboom aloes, whose peeling, creamy-coloured trunks are topped by a large canopy of typically spiky aloe leaves, and candelabra-like yellow flowers which attract sunbirds, starlings and weavers. Found on the hot, northern slopes of the mountains in this area are 'halfmens' plants, *Pachypodium namaquanum*. Hottentot stories tell us that these strange succulent trees are half human and half plant, and indeed from afar they do startlingly resemble human forms, with their small, crinkly crowns always pointing towards the sun.

When Karl Thunberg travelled through the arid west, he spent much of his time in the Gifberg mountains, above Vanrhynsdorp. On the well-watered summit plateau of these outliers of the Cape Fold mountains, he found the northernmost extension of the fynbos flora. He identified many fynbos species here, including the original and widespread sugarbush, *Protea repens*. Thunberg called this plant *mellifera*, or honeybearing; it is much favoured by nectar-drinking creatures and has also long been used by rural people as a source of sweetener called 'bossiestroop' ('wild syrup', or, literally, 'little bush syrup'). The father of modern taxonomy, Linnaeus, had earlier given this plant a specific name meaning 'creeping' after being misled by an inaccurate illustration.

North of Springbok and receding into a great loop made by the Orange River, is one of the most inaccessible and hostile areas on the subcontinent, rivalled only by the barren Namib Desert. This is the Richtersveld mountainland, where even four-wheel-drive vehicles have short life spans. The jarring corrugations of its roads seem to be miniatures of the ranks of quartzite and granite mountains that turn the Richtersveld into a moonscape, similar to those burning, burnished and gnarled mountainlands of the Kaokoveld, the Swakop and Kuiseb canyons in Namibia. The mountains here, such as the Rosyntjieberg with its maze of gullies and scars which give it the texture of a giant raisin, are, however, generally more prominent than those in Namibia.

This place is filled with grandeur and pathos – the landscapes are certainly grand, but the plants, the animals and the small human settlements, such as Eksteenfontein, and the quaintly named Lekkersing, seem like pitiful flotsam in this unfriendly land. The valley floors are baked hard and the rough hillsides all but devoid of vegetation, other than a few weird, small plants. The feeling of being the only person ever to see this remote area is common to those who manage to get there. But plans are afoot to proclaim a national park in the Richtersveld; people are still not likely to come here in droves, but those who do will be rewarded with a unique experience of true wilderness.

Above: *A* ruschia *plant in bloom – a typical succulent of the Karoo. The Karoo is a wonderland of succulent plants, and botanists have yet to identify them all. Some look exactly like the pebbles among which they grow. In the family* Mesembryanthemaceae *alone, of which this* ruschia *is a member, there are over 2 000 species.*

Orange Free State

Previous pages: *Lesser flamingoes feed at Flamingo Pan near Welkom. These birds filter algae from the pan by floating their cork-like beaks on the surface. Their tongues act like hydraulic pumps, sucking in the nutrient-rich water, which is then filtered through a fine mesh in the beak. The tongue's pumping action then forces the water out again.*

Left: *The Orange Free State – this province is South Africa's 'mealie basket'. Maize meal is the staple diet of most of the country's inhabitants.*

Right above: *Cumulo-nimbus storm clouds build over Allemanskraal Dam in the Willem Pretorius Game Reserve. Most of the rain that falls on the Highveld grasslands comes in the form of summer afternoon cloudbursts from these thermally-developed clouds.*

Right below: *Although most of the Orange Free State consists of flat grasslands, cultivated fields and scattered, flat-topped koppies, its eastern border abuts the Maluti and Thaba Putsoa mountains of Lesotho. In the north-eastern corner lies the Golden Gate Highlands National Park; the basalt-capped sandstone highlands seen here are the foothills of the Drakensberg.*

South Africa's land-locked Orange Free State province is the brunt of many jokes, particularly concerning the absolute flatness of so much of it. While it is true that the entire province consists of horizontally bedded Karoo Supergroup rocks, its north-eastern border includes some of the highest peaks on the subcontinent. The border area with Lesotho, around Ladybrand, is backed by the massive Thaba Putsoa mountains, while the gem of the province is the protected mountain-land of the Little Caledon River catchment area that lies at the north-eastern corner of the Drakensberg.

Almost the entire surface of the Golden Gate Highlands National Park consists of the highly erodable Cave Sandstones. The park is like an extensive maze, which the Little Caledon River and its tributaries have cut into the sandstone and the even softer Red Bed deposits that underlie it. The Red Beds are undercut everywhere to form caves and parabolic overhangs, like the Mushroom Rocks formation that seem to hang suspended over the roadway, just north of Glen Reenen camp.

The Little Caledon River has cut itself a deep gorge, leaving great rock portals protruding into the river valley. Interlocking gateways with names like the Brandwag (sentinel) and Gladstone's Nose characterize the park. The normally creamy-white sandstone bastions have been tinted copper and red by oxidation of the exposed rock; sunset throws a fiery light onto the west-facing walls. The park is encircled by pyramidal basalt peaks, such as Generaals Kop, Ribbokkop and Wodehouse Kop – remnants of the Stormberg volcanic layer that once covered most of Natal, Lesotho and the Orange Free State.

The point at which the Little Caledon River joins its parent, the Caledon River, marks the fertile valley that became the ancestral home of Chief Moshesh, founder of the modern Basotho nation. He

retreated here with the vagabonds and refugees of the bloody Difa-qane wars which changed the face of the southern African interior. First Thaba Ntsu and then the more impressive Thaba Bosiu – the mountain of the night – were used as natural fortresses to repulse fierce Zulu and Matabele invasions. Later still, sieges and attacks by Boer commandos and British forces failed to dislodge the emergent Basotho nation and their wily, diplomatic leader from their mountain kingdom.

The Voortrekkers, under the leadership of Piet Retief, outspanned in the vicinity of the present park and hunted, departing when their wagons were heavily laden with biltong from eland and wildebeest, blesbok, springbok and rhebok, mountain reedbuck and duiker. The skins from these animals would have been piled on the floors of the wagons, among lion and leopard hides, perhaps cheetah and serval skins too. Years later, the Boer farmers who settled in the fertile valleys hereabouts, still shot lions by the score. Today, however, the Golden Gate game reserve is too small to support a wildlife

Below: *Gladstone's Nose – the whimsical name given to the sandstone tower on the left – sniffs over a dam on the Little Caledon River. This river and its tributaries have carved out the soft rock in the Golden Gate Highlands National Park to form the so-called gates and other overhanging formations.*

ecosystem complete with large predators. Instead, the emphasis here is on outdoor recreation, with many walks and trails, where stealthy hikers can observe the reintroduced game at close range.

The South African War battle site of Magersfontein lies just within the Cape provincial boundary – a randomly drawn line that was one of the causes of that war. When diamonds were discovered around Kimberley, just within the borders of the Boer republic of the Orange Free State, the Cape colonial government simply drew a new border line so as to capture the major diamond fields. During the early days of the war, the Highland Brigade marched across hundreds of kilometres of the dolerite-blackened northern Cape veld, only to be cut down by the merciless hail of 6 000 Boer rifles. The Boer forces, under the command of generals Cronje and De la Rey, took the British troops by surprise, being concealed in trenches along the base of the Magersfontien ridge. The British had thought to dislodge the Boers from the crest of the ridge with artillery fire, but lost the battle, as well as 900 troops out of total force of 3 500.

One of the jokes about the Orange Free State recalls that when the Voortrekkers reached its flat grass plains, they came upon a signpost. The sign informed those who sought tropical seas, dreams and relaxation to turn right to Natal, while those who wanted wealth and industry were to carry on straight ahead to the Transvaal – and those who could not read stayed put and founded Bloemfontein. Yet this became a beautiful city, the capital of the most enlightened of the Boer republics, presided over by learned men like President Steyn and President Brand.

The northern Orange Free State farmers have since turned the country's finest grazing lands into the nation's breadbasket, where endless ranks of maize and sunflowers ripen in the Highveld sunshine. While the Great Karoo scrublands formerly terminated along the Orange River, decades of overstocking by the Free State's southern sheep farmers have allowed these semi-desert conditions to creep northwards and eastwards into the province, blending imperceptibly with the grasslands.

Above: *In spring a stalk of the plant* Brunsvigia radulosa *pushes up through the ground from a football-sized bulb. Arms then grow out from the stalk and flower, to form this chandelier of cerise blooms. When it dries out, the spherical, spiked ball detaches itself and rolls across the Highveld, spreading its seeds.*

The Eastern Cape and Transkei

In 1859 the regional magistrate of the southern Transkei area, Lieutenant (later General) Colley, was surveying the district. On peering down into one of the many convoluted river valleys that cut through the country, he is reputed to have said 'My, how it wobbles'. Upon this, one of his aides replied: 'Yes, it colleywobbles' and that name, The Colleywobbles, has stuck for the section of the Mbashe River that twists and doubles back, cutting a spectacular gorge. The Mbashe, however, is but one of the many rivers that cut deeply through the knobbly land, leaping over high falls on their rush through forests down to the coastal plains, there fanning out into wide, tranquil estuaries and mangrove swamps where they meet the sea. The eastern Cape and Transkei is mostly low, rolling country- side, where traditional clay and grass huts cling to the slopes of the hills like the barnacles that cling to its rocky shores.

The geology of the region is much the same as that of the greater Karoo area, comprising largely Karoo Supergroup rocks. In many places, however, the coastal margin is covered with marine and allu- vial sandy deposits, giving rise to the famous beaches of Algoa Bay, St Francis Bay and Jeffreys Bay, Port Alfred and East London. Rocky beaches are formed by protruding arms of Beaufort Group rocks, or the harder dolerite deposits of the Stormberg Group that form dra- matic sea cliffs north of Port St Johns.

Previous pages: *The tip of Cathedral Rock looms up in a cleft in the cliffs north of Port St Johns. This is the wildest part of the Wild Coast, where the sea has carved arches and tunnels into the cliffs and high sea stacks, and waterfalls plunge 60 metres into pounding surf.*

Left: *An isolated road snakes its way through the Baviaanskloof mountains in the eastern Cape. A new wilderness area has recently been proclaimed in these rugged mountains.*

Below: *A beach at Port Alfred. For many years attempts were made to turn this into a commercial harbour to serve the 1820 Settler farming community of the eastern Cape. The nearby Kowie River seemed to offer a wide and deep draught for ships, but strong westerly winds, which built these shifting dunes, pushed ships onto the sandbars in the mouth. Far-off (by ox-wagon standards) Port Elizabeth grew to become the major port in the region instead.*

Above: *Transkei's Wild Coast was not so named for its obviously rocky and hazardous shores, nor for the giant freak waves that build up off the narrow continental shelf and engulf large ships. It was the 'wildness' of the indigenous people who intimidated shipwreck survivors of the sixteenth and seventeeth centuries that gave the place its name.*

Hard dolerite sills that have been intruded into softer shales resist erosion by the myriad rivers and streams that rush down from the Transkei hinterland and race to the coast. These sills form the lips of the many waterfalls that punctuate the rivers. In some cases, where the dolerite has resisted the jackhammer waves, rivers plunge directly over the cliffs into the sea. Near the sea-sculpted Cathedral Rocks – twin stacks complete with aisles, spires and flying buttresses – the thundering Mfihlelo River plunges 160 metres into the surging swells below.

An equally spectacular dolerite formation is seen at the famous Hole-in-the-Wall resort, where the combined forces of river and wave erosion have severed a formerly continuous cliffline, to create a whale-back island with a barrel vault through its centre. This is the Hole-in-the-Wall, through which the surf is funnelled in a jet-like stream.

It is believed that Port St Johns was named after the Portuguese caravel the *São João* which foundered in 1552 just south of the place where the mighty Mzimvubu River has cut twin portals through a great, forested headland to form the Gates of St John. The Pondos called this river 'the home of the hippopotomus', but white hunters of the 19th-century soon shot out all the hippos and crocodiles from the river, as well as the elephants and other game that teemed in the lush valley of the Mzimvubu River. The quaint town of Port St Johns is a mixture of old colonial splendour gone to seed and of Third World indifference. It is a colourful combination of elements: people, river, sea and flower-festooned forests that seem eager to claim back what the white colonists fought so hard to wrestle from the African wilderness.

The British settlers who landed at Algoa Bay in 1820, were settled in the war-torn buffer zone between the Sundays and Great Fish

rivers of the eastern Cape. This was the time of the frontier warfare, when British forces were employed in a long and bitter series of battles and skirmishes against Xhosa tribes, which were slowly advancing south-westwards, over the limits of the Cape colony's land. By whites, this part of the the eastern Cape, with its cultural focus at Grahamstown, is often called 'Settler Country', for here the British settlers carved a niche for themselves against great adversity. Towns like Bathurst, Salem, Southwell and Grahamstown still strongly reflect the legacy of these uprooted Europeans. The old stone churches, inns and whitewashed farmhouses, water mills, elegant townhouses and administrative buildings that remain infuse the area with a sense of history and cultural determination. A line of forts was built by the British forces along this 'eastern frontier', and many of these square stone blockhouses still stand. Starting on Gunfire Hill above Grahamstown, they follow the high ground along the Great Fish River Valley, all the way to Fort Beaufort.

Neither black nor white settlers bothered to tame the dense bushveld between the Suurberg mountains, the Sundays River and Algoa Bay, even though this was the very interface of conflict between these two land-hungry peoples. The Addo bush was so thick that it harboured elephant herds right until the beginning of 1919, when Major P. J. Pretorius, a hero of the Great War, was commissioned to shoot the crop-raiding animals.

By the end of that year there were only 16 elephants left in the Addo bush, for Major Pretorius was a brave and determined, if misguided, man, and an excellent shot. Fears then arose, however, that these great animals would go the way of the quagga and the bluebuck – to extinction. In 1931 the hunt was called off and the Addo Elephant National Park was proclaimed. At that time only 11 elephants were left there, but they quickly multiplied, numbering 35 in 1964 and 120 by 1986.

The park protected not only the elephant, but also the last of the Cape's buffalo which had managed to escape persecution. The dry, hot Addo bush comprises mainly Karooboerboon trees (*Schotia afra*), small, pale-barked trees with finefeathered leaves and showy red flowers; the fleshy-leaved spekboom (*Portulacaria afra*) shrub with soft wood much loved by sheep and browsing game, the leaves of which are also eaten by black women when they have insufficient milk for their babies; and the dense and twiggy common guarri bush (*Euclea undulata*).

Inland of Addo and Grahamstown is the historic university town of Alice, where London missionaries established the Lovedale Missionary College and the first printing press in southern Africa. The college became Fort Hare University and the Lovedale Press gave rise to a proud tradition of black journalism and education in general that continues today. From the dusty plain of Fort Beaufort to Alice, the Hogsback mountains rise into the crisp air of the subcontinent's southernmost afro-alpine mountain enclave. On top of the dolerite Hogsback crests are found typical alpine heathlands; below this is a fynbos belt where chest-high erica and protea plants form impenetrable thickets; further below this are temperate yellowwood forests that rival the Tsitsikamma's famous woods.

Cascades, such as the Bridal Veil, Swallowtail and Madonna and Child waterfalls, plunge over precipices within the forests, where cosy mountain inns offer warmth and wholesome country fare. The Hogsback is part of the greater Amatola or Winterberg range, which stretches across the northern Ciskei to the Katberg mountain complex. Andrew Geddes Bain built the Katberg Pass through these sharp peaks, which seem to carve at the eggshell-blue sky like sharpened knives. In winter the Amatola range lies covered in snow and its waterfalls freeze solid, while in summer the mountains are dusted with the bright blooms of everlastings.

Between the golden arcs of St Francis Bay and Algoa Bay, the Cape Fold mountains finally peter out; the fynbos-sprinkled slopes of the Suurberg range blend into the thorn bushveld and sour grasslands just west of Grahamstown. Ecologists call this area 'the eastern Cape tension zone' because it is the meeting place of the fynbos, grassland, savanna, afro-montane and subtropical lowland forest ecosystems. The climate here is equally variable, leading a local scribe to write: 'The vernal joys of Grahamstown are something to remember, spring comes not once, but four times 'twixt mid-June and November'.

Above: *Dense euphorbia forest covers the hot slopes in the Great Fish River Valley that marks the southern boundary of Ciskei. The veld type is Valley Bushveld and is considered a southern form of the African savanna that stretches up into east Africa.*

Natal and the
Drakensberg

At the southern end of the Drakensberg, in Lesotho's Sehlaba-Thebe National Park, a cloud-flecked mountain with three connected peaks is reflected in the park's many tarns. The mountain is appropriately called Thaba Ntsu, the Mountain of the Lammergeier, for this highland wilderness is the subcontinent's only remaining sanctuary of the lammergeier, or bearded vulture. This magnificent golden-plumed bird, half eagle and half vulture, relies on a diet of bone fragments from carrion and the scraps left by Lesotho's semi-nomadic herders. Like the American condor the lammergeier is threatened by its shrinking habitat, and in its area is considered one of the most endangered bird species.

The other name by which the Drakensberg's southernmost mountain is known is the Three Bushmen. The cracked basalt crests sweep up from the source of the Bushman's River and from Bushman's Nek Pass, through which the last Bushmen cattle raids were conducted during the 1870s. Sehlaba-Thebe aptly means 'the shield', as the park is a plateau, raised on a three-sided pedestal of sandstone cliffs, called the Little Berg. Along its western boundary the plateau adjoins the Drakensberg Escarpment wall. The large sandstone caves which pock these cliffs were the homes of Bushmen clans for thousands of years, before the Difaqane wars and the subsequent arrival of white hunters and farmers squeezed them out.

However, in the caves here and throughout the Drakensberg these little yellow people, often hunted down and shot as 'vermin' by settlers and adventurers, left behind a legacy of rock art which tells of their lives, their hunting-orientated mythology and their poetry, and which testifies to their great skill as artists. The fast-fading paintings are considered to be the finest collection of rock art in the world. The stylistic drawings capture the essence of moving people and animals with an unequalled grace. The last known remaining Bushman in Natal was shot in the Giant's Castle area, shortly before a game reserve was proclaimed there to protect the Drakensberg's last eland herds. This individual was also probably their last great artist, for around his waist was found a belt of small antelope horns, stuffed with the pigments he mixed with egg white, animal fat and aloe juice, and the shredded twigs that were his brushes.

The high basalt walls of the Drakensberg were originally formed by massive outpourings of lava that brought the Karoo's Stormberg geological period to a close. The volcanic eruptions began about 180 million years ago and carried on successively for the next 30 million

Previous pages: Early morning brings a mist to the valleys in the Hluhluwe Game Reserve in Zululand. Here in Natal are found some of the oldest nature reserves in southern Africa, some of them dating back to the days of the Zulu king Shaka, who decreed them royal hunting grounds and forests.

Above: *Devil's Tooth sticks up between the Inner and Outer Towers of the Amphitheatre's Eastern Buttress in the Drakensberg.*

years or so, in the most spectacular pyrotechnical display the earth has experienced. It formed a sheet of basalt covering most of the Karoo Basin, which at its thickest lay some 10 kilometres deep. During subsequent storms and high rainfall, the basalt sheet was whittled away at its outer edges, and today all that remains are the castellated walls of the Natal Drakensberg and the crinkled, green Thaba Putsoa and Maluti highlands of Lesotho.

Giant's Castle Peak (3 316 metres) is the highest peak standing apart from the main wall of mountains. The narrow ridge from which it rises protrudes out from the escarpment for four kilometres, forming a pivot between the northern and southern parts of the 'Berg. While the southern section of the range is generally as high as the northern, it is not as dramatic and has few outstanding features. North of Giant's Castle, however, the mountains are punctuated by five regularly spaced masses of jagged peaks and towers, steep

Above: *Giant's Castle is the name given to the highest peak on this ridge which juts out for four kilometres from the main escarpment, marking the midpoint of the Drakensberg range.*

Below: *Between the point where the Thukela River plunges over the Drakensberg, and where it cuts a cavernous gorge through the underlying sandstone beds, the river rushes through a boulder-cluttered avenue. The surrounding curved walls of the Amphitheatre seem to arch right over the scene.*

passes that thread their way up precipitous gullies, and sweeping ramparts.

First are the Injasuti Triplets – awesome turrets of rock that stand out from the Trojan Wall. Behind the Triplets the escarpment rises to an altitude of 3 450 metres; this is Mafadi Peak – the highest peak of the Drakensberg. The Trojan Wall leads on to the Old Woman Grinding Corn and Champagne Castle, where the eye sweeps up the steep and jagged Cathkin Ridge to the imposing Cathkin Peak which the Zulus call 'make room for him' – Mdedelelo, the bully. Rising from a knife edge between Champagne Castle (3 377 metres) and Cathkin Peak, the ominous Monk's Cowl looms up through swirling mists. The Cowl has claimed the lives of more rock climbers than any other peak in the 'Berg, and yet still they return to defy its treachery.

The Cathedral Range forms a transept of some four kilometres to the escarpment, as does Giant's Ridge, and culminates at Cathedral Peak, supported by the Bell, the Horns, the Chessmen and the Mitre, while rising up from the Tseketseke Valley in the Cathedral's shadow, the Column and the Pyramid pierce the sky. North of Cathedral, the Saddle's twin flanks frame Mnweni – most aptly named the 'place of fingers', with its Needles, Pinnacles, Rockeries, Abbey and Organ Pipes. These chiselled formations stand out in ragged ranks, bank upon bank of fluted rock with overreaching buttresses, needle-sharp spires and massive towers. The Zulus call this mountain range Quathlamba, 'the barrier of spears'.

At its northern end, the Amphitheatre and Sentinel stand like bookends to support the Drakensberg's massed peaks. From base to summit, this five-kilometre-long wall represents the greatest natural drop and the most dramatic vista in all of southern Africa. The Thukela River rises on the slopes of Mont-aux-Sources some two kilometres behind the escarpment wall, and plummets in three giant leaps five hundred metres down the Amphitheatre's face, into the

Below: *Below the high ramparts of the 'Berg, the grassy hills of Giant's Castle were proclaimed a game reserve to protect the dwindling herds of eland here at the beginning of this century. These massive antelope were the most important animal in the lives of Bushmen, who for centuries used the many surrounding caves as seasonal shelters.*

Above: *The Mzimkulu River rises in the Drakensberg just south of Sani Pass and snakes through the rolling Natal Midlands. The famous book by Alan Paton, 'Cry the Beloved Country', begins with a description of the river as it flows through these hills.*

Right: *The Howick Falls exploit a structural defect in a dolerite sill by creating a display of liquid force and elegance along the Mgeni River.*

Previous pages: *The Amphitheatre forms a majestic backdrop to the Thukela River valley. The river rises on the slopes of Mont-aux-Sources, set above and behind this basalt castle, and then plunges over the escarpment in three magnificent leaps before flowing out across Natal.*

polished tunnels and forested shoulders of the Thukela Gorge.

From its gushing passage through the gorge, the youthful river gurgles down its valley with braided pebble channels, before ambling out across the wide open grasslands of the Natal Midlands. Within the Drakensberg's generous catchment bowls rise many of Natal's principal rivers, such as the Mkomazi and Mzimkulu. Where the Howick Falls plunge from a tributary into the Mgeni River, the Midlands drop into the lowveld savanna of Natal's subtropical coastal belt. Here the Mgeni winds its way through the Valley of a Thousand Hills, and then forms a double estuary at Durban's Blue Lagoon.

Broadening northwards, the lowveld rolls on into the wooded hills of Zululand, where a number of famous game reserves, such as Mkuze, Umfolozi and Hluhluwe, protect the world's most important breeding herds of both white and black rhinoceroses. Wilderness trails through these reserves allow hikers to experience true African wilderness conditions, where large game, including predators, may be encountered on foot.

Ndumu Game Reserve is less known and its facilities are more basic than the others, but only the Okavango Delta rivals this small sanctuary for its prolific birdlife. Some 416 species (nearly half of the total found in southern Africa) have been recorded in the reserve,

Above: *Twilight over Richards Bay on the Zululand coast. When the new harbour was built here in the early 1970s, careful planning preserved the ecologically-sensitive shallows, while developing the deeper channels. While this has allowed the much-reduced mangrove swamps on the southern shore to revive, subsequent canalization of the Mhlatuze swamp, and the cultivation of sugarcane has led to the silting up of the protected part of the estuary.*

including east African species such as the African broadbill and yellow-spotted nicator. These exotic species use the coastal tropical forests as a 'habitat corridor' down which to travel. Ndumu is also the southernmost haunt of the rare palmnut vulture, which feeds mainly on the husks of the thinly distributed Kosi palm, as well as the fruit of wild date palms. On the Ndumu River floodplain are found many species of waterfowl, large waders such as black herons, fish eagles and nocturnal Pel's fishing owls. The evergreen scrub forests and swamp grasslands provide habitats for game species, such as nyala and bushbuck, elusive duiker and tiny suni antelope, reedbuck, zebra, and black and white rhino.

On Zululand's coastal plain there are numerous estuarine and freshwater lake systems, the largest of which is the St Lucia Estuary. The estuary mouth is fed directly by the Mfolozi and Msunduze rivers, while the extensive lake area behind the dunes is fed more slowly by the waters of the Mkuze, Hluhluwe and several lesser rivers that are filtered through broad swamplands. The estuary mouth is narrow while the 'lake' area broadens northwards for 60 kilometres; its ecology is delicately balanced between fresh and marine water

Below: *Lake St Lucia is actually a huge estuary, the largest in southern Africa, and much of its shore and water is protected area. Preserved habitats include the estuary itself, freshwater swamplands, coastal sub-tropical forest and savanna grasslands. Large birds such as various eagles, flamingoes, herons and other large waders are most conspicuous, but St Lucia protects predominantly the crocodiles and hippos that live in the water and on the more remote banks.*

systems, between tropical and sub-tropical biological zones and between marginal sugarcane lands, plantations and holiday resorts, and the sanctuary of four adjacent game reserves.

Lake St Lucia is cut off from the sea by the world's highest coastal dunes which are now stabilized by climax dune forest. The dune and acacia woodlands are a place of venomous snakes. Forest cobras slither through dune forests, green mambas keep mainly to the trees, while Mozambique spitting cobras keep to the forest edge. Among the floor litter lives one of the most visually stunning and lethal of all snakes, the limb-thick gaboon viper with its bright geometric camouflage patterns.

The savanna woodlands are the habitat of black mambas, which rival the gaboon viper for its evil reputation, as well as boomslangs and vine snakes, Egyptian cobras and puff-adders. St Lucia is mainly a hippopotomus and crocodile reserve, but other large mammals present include buffalo, zebra and the largest concentration of reedbuck in Africa. Eagles, pelicans and flamingoes are the most conspicuous of St Lucia's prolific birdlife. Long-crested eagles with their characteristic head plumes can often be seen perching on telephone

Above: *The land near Rorkes Drift, scene of one of the most bloody and heroic battles in the history of the region. In January of 1879, British forces under Lord Chelmsford camped in the area as a prelude to an invasion of Zululand. As they camped below Isandlwana hill they were ambushed and humiliated by a Zulu impi. Meanwhile, a small force of 139 British soldiers was stationed in the Swedish Mission here at Rorke's Drift. They were attacked in the late afternoon by two Zulu regiments. The attack lasted 12 hours, during which 15 British and 400 Zulu soldiers were killed – but the mission was successfully defended, and the most Victoria Crosses for any one battle were awarded to the defending garrison.*

poles on the St Lucia road bridge, crowned eagles sometimes soar high above the forests, while fish eagles and ospreys flap lazily across the estuary.

The Kosi Bay coastal lakes which occupy the north-eastern corner of Zululand, resemble the Wilderness Lakes complex in their formation. The lake complex consists of four freshwater lakes, with one emptying into the sea through a narrow but permanent mouth. This lake is known as Kosi Bay and it is inhabited by crocodiles and hippos, as well as Zambezi sharks which occasionally venture into the mouth.

A four-wheel-drive vehicle is necessary to cross the swampy and sandy ground in the Kosi area, but once at the reserve, one is rewarded by the astounding diversity of ecosystems: over 250 bird species inhabit the aquatic and forest habitats; thick mangrove swamps surround the open estuary, where all species of mangrove forest trees are present in healthy populations, as well the crabs and other specialized creatures adapted to live in the glutinuous mud

banks; and the forested dunes lead down to the tropical beaches of Maputoland where loggerhead and leatherback turtles breed annually.

Between here and Cape Vidal, game fishermen bag sailfish and fierce fighting marlin or sleek barracuda. Divers explore the coral reefs where moray eels lurk in lobster holes among tentacled anemones, spiky sea-urchins, starfish and brilliant, mantled molluscs. Deadly stonefish lie camouflaged in the shallow pools, whereas brightly coloured scorpion fish advertize their danger flamboyantly, their poison-tipped spines waving from flag-like fins. In and out of the coral caverns swim parrot fish, clown fish and moorish idols, with their pendant dorsal fins. Along the shore one can spend hours fossicking for polished cowrie and cone shells, corals, ribbed harp shells, spiralling turret shells and delicate venus combs. At full moon the tide is spring low, and this is the time to take torch and 'takkies' and explore the exposed reefs when all these creatures can be seen feeding in their luminous finery.

Above: *Like biltong and boerewors, cycads are a uniquely South African feature, and all members of the genus* Encephalartos *are strictly protected. Plants such as this* E. natalensis *are botanically fascinating in that they are 'living fossils', being the most primitive of seed-bearing plants. They belong to an ancient order that flourished between 50 and 60 million years ago.*

Lesotho and Swaziland

Previous pages: *A three-peaked mountain marks the southern end of the Drakensberg Escarpment: Thaba Ntsu – home of the lammergeier, or bearded vulture. These basalt battlements stand guard over Lesotho's Sehlaba-Thebe National Park. They stand at the head of the Bushman's River valley and pass, and are also known as the Three Bushmen, and , perhaps less appropriately, as the Devil's Knuckles.*

Above: *Basalt is formed when lava is extruded on the surface where it cools relatively quickly, while dolerite comes from the same source but is intruded between subterranean layers of rock. Here it cools very slowly to form iron-hard sills and dykes (depending on whether it lies horizontally of vertically). Where the surrounding rocks have been stripped away, the dolerite resists these forces, forming ridges or flat-topped hills, or waterfalls where rivers could not cut through the rock. The Tsoelike River plunges over a dolerite sill in the southern Drakensberg foothills in Lesotho.*

Lesotho and Swaziland are both small, landlocked kingdoms, scenic jewels where traditional African lifestyles persist among the mountains and forest, the cultivated valleys and the pastures. Both countries are essentially mountainlands with countless waterfalls and tempting peaks to explore.

Lesotho is often called the 'kingdom in the sky'; its crinkled hills and plateaux resemble those of Tibet in their remoteness and the isolated pastoral lifestyle still practised there resembles that of the Tibetans. Swaziland is a more gentle, rolling land, a genuine monarchy, ruled by the young King Mswati III.

Swaziland falls into the physiographical region called the Eastern Plateau Slopes. This region lies west of the Great Escarpment and east of the Mozambique Coastal Plain. The eastern section is rolling mountainous country, with a pleasant climate of warm summers and crisp, sunny winters. The western lowveld, however, is a dusty and hot, malaria-plagued savanna which extends into the Transvaal Lowveld.

Vigorous stream action along the edge of the escarpment is the architect of the country's rolling topography . The Komati River is fed by the many streams which rise in the Eastern Transvaal Escarpment near Waterval-Boven. From there the Komati cuts a wide and deep valley right through Swaziland's north-western mountains to connect the lowveld on either side, then again it cuts through the Lebombo mountains, finding its way across Mozambique's coastal plain and into the swamplands around Maputo Bay.

The bumpy north-western corner of Swaziland is part of a geological unit known as the Barberton Mountainland. Rocks of the Onverwacht, Figtree and Moodies systems are among the oldest on earth and were laid down on top of the earth's original crust. But this crust was too thin to support the later deposits, and so it disintegrated beneath the surface. Although orginally a hotchpotch of sediments, these Fundamental Complex rocks have now been mostly altered to form schists and gneisses, cherts, shales and quartzites. They have been dated at about 3,5 billion years old, while the earth is generally regarded as being another billion years or so older.

The most fascinating feature of these rocks is that they contain evidence of the oldest known life on earth. The remains of rod-like micro-organisms, probably bacterial, have been found in the least metamorphosed cherts of the Onverwacht and Figtree groups, dated at about 3 400 million years old. Stromatolites of blue-green algae from rocks of a slightly younger age have also been found in this area.

The Fundamental Complex rocks are surrounded by intrusions known as the Older Granites, which are indicative of long periods of geological stability. Geologists divide southern Africa up into relatively stable 'cratons', separated by unstable 'mobile belts'. Swazi-

Above: *Sehlaba-Thebe, or 'the shield' is the widest section of the Little Berg intermediate plateau, raised above the the rest of this step-like formation that abuts the main Drakensberg Escarpment. This shield is dotted with large but shallow tarns, meandering streams and ox-bow lakes. This haunt of playful otters is, due to its unique topography, the home of some rare endemic plant species.*

land falls entirely within the Kaapvaal Craton, as do the southern and central Transvaal, northern Natal and Orange Free State and the north-eastern Cape. Other cratons are the Richtersveld, Zimbabwe and Angolan, while there are the Cape Fold, Damara, Namaqualand, Natal, Mozambique, Limpopo and Zambezi mobile belts. A careful examination of a geological map will reveal that all the major rivers of southern Africa find their way into the fault lines of these mobile belts.

The basaltic Lebombo mountains divide Swaziland from Mozambique and are part of the Stormberg volcanics, but are slightly younger than Lesotho's smothering of Drakensberg basalts. Lesotho stands like a castle above the rest of southern Africa, protected from erosion by this thick laval skin – the last remaining block of a volcanic sheet that once lay over much of southern Africa. Except for the heavily populated, low lying Caledon and Telle river valleys, the entire country is covered by alpine grasslands and heaths.

Three mountain axes define this mountain wilderness, all radiating out from the northernmost corner. In the east the Drakensberg

Previous pages: *Lesotho is a very rugged, elevated country, buttressed on all sides by high mountain ranges. This mountain kingdom sits in the centre of South Africa like a crown, which is an appropriate metaphor for one of the continent's few remaining monarchies. The Drakensberg basalts, which cover more than two-thirds of the country, have been sliced into tiny pieces by thousands of rivers and streams, exposing the soft Cave Sandstone, and even softer Red Beds sandstones beneath.*

Above: *The Kingdom of Swaziland, the other monarchy in southern Africa, is divided roughly between an eastern montane and a western lowland savanna region. Between the two, and a short way from the capital city Mbabane, lies Mlilwane Wildlife Sanctuary. This a small but well-run reserve where large game, excluding large predators, can be viewed from vehicles or on foot.*

Right: *A view of Mlilwane, showing the two main ecosystems within the park and Swaziland itself. Open savanna rolls up to the distant green hills, while plantations of exotic trees stand between the two. Timber from the mountain plantations and tourism are the country's most important industries.*

Above: *Between the dusty Swaziland lowveld, and the hot Mozambique coastal plain, are the Lebombo mountains. These basalt hills run as a thin line starting inland in northern Zululand, up the eastern margin of Swaziland and the eastern Transvaal, making a detour up the Limpopo River Valley, then along the south-eastern border of Zimbabwe. From here they tend to the north-east into Mozambique and terminate in the Lupata district in a hook-shaped formation. This picture was taken in Swaziland's Ndzindza Nature Reserve.*

Escarpment fades into the southern Border Range somewhere around Ramatsiliso's Gate. Thaba Ntlenyana (3 482 metres), the highest peak in southern Africa, appears as nothing more than a con-ical plateau behind the escarpment wall. In the west the Orange Free State plains sweep up to the hazy 'Blue mountains' – the Thaba Put-soa and Maluti ranges. The Senqu (Orange) and Senqunyane rivers cut deep valleys to leave the Central Range rising up from the surrounding, convoluted countryside.

This crown of mountains is a hiker's paradise, and nowhere more so than the Central Range. Villagers in this river-sliced region are visited only by the most tenacious mountaineers, by pony trekkers, Peace Corps workers and missionaries. However, construction has already begun on the Lesotho Highlands Water Scheme which will bring a system of hydro-electric dams, paved roads, electricity and associated new towns to this incomparable mountaineering wilderness. Although Lesotho will benefit financially from the South African-financed scheme, no-one has yet decided what to do with the peasants whose fields and villages are to be inundated by the dam waters.

Notwithstanding the bitter weather, winter in Lesotho is the sunny season, for during the summer months the hills and valleys are often shrouded in mist or pelted by thunderstorms. Snow is likely to fall at any time during the autumn and winter, and temperatures at night freeze waterfalls and rivers, as well as unprepared

campers. There is a seemingly endless network of paths across the highlands, mostly following dolerite dykes which are even and resistant to erosion, but because the lie of the land is so complex, it is easy to get lost in the central region. Luckily though, herdsmen and riders in traditional blankets and Basotho hats are nearly always friendly and will guide one on to the next occupied village or passable river crossing.

Along the country's lower western margin, the myriad streams have sliced deeply into soft Cave Sandstone and Red Bed layers that underlie the basalt layer. The caves that are a feature of these valleys are famous for their unusual Bushman paintings which include depictions of blue cranes and large predators, dancing and hunting scenes. Perhaps even more interesting are the footprints and fossil bones of mammal-like reptiles (incorrectly called dinosaurs) of the Karoo period that made their last stand here before the fury of the Stormberg volcanic period obliterated almost everything in the Karoo Basin.

Above: Protea subvestita, *one of the common flowering bushes which grow around an altitude of 2 000 metres in the Drakensberg and eastern Lesotho. There are five species of Protea found in the Drakensberg, three of which, including this one, are endemic.*

Eastern Transvaal

Previous pages: *Rain and mist lie over the eastern Transvaal highlands most days of the year, and rainbows frequently bathe the hills in soft, rain-washed hues.*

Left: *The road that winds along the edge of the Blyde River Canyon was built specially to make this area more accessible for sightseeing and other recreational activities. The canyon, the surrounding highland plateau, the deep gorges, and the remote wilderness areas of the Eastern Transvaal Escarpment offer a range of outdoor recreation opportunities, from historical sightseeing to the most demanding mountaineering.*

Above: *Below Swadeni, near the mouth of the canyon, is the Blydepoort Dam. Wild life of the Lowveld moves up the canyon between the massive rock towers and into the mountainlands here.*

Two very different landscapes rub shoulders in the eastern Transvaal, connected by a wall of glass-hard quartzite 1 000 metres high. On the one side there are the verdant cool valleys of the Highveld plateau around Sabie and Pilgrim's Rest, the mist-soaked mountain ridges and impenetrable kloofs of the Downs and Wolkberg wilderness areas, where mountain streams become thundering cataracts and waterfalls within the forested gorges. On the other side is the stiflingly hot Lowveld bush that lies below this wall and stretches eastwards all the way to the Indian Ocean and up into east Africa. This malaria-infested plain, pimpled with granite koppies, is an endless expanse of mopane woodlands, tall grass savanna, acacia and combretum thickets, monumental baobabs, wild animals, heat and dust.

The Great Escarpment which forms the geological interface be-

Above: *In the gorges and valleys of the eastern Transvaal are many grand waterfalls. The gold rush here in the 1870s attracted prospectors and fortune-seekers from all over Europe, especially the economically-depressed areas of Scotland and Ireland. The Mac-Mac Falls (seen here) were jocularly named after the many Scottish and Irish prospectors who were active in the area.*

Right: *The Long Tom Pass near Blydepoort. During the South African War, the Boer artillery positioned a large-calibre cannon here which they called 'Long Tom'. Towards the end of the war the British also dragged big guns up these rugged heights, and as the Boers retreated eastwards, the two opposing forces pounded each other across the intervening hills and valleys. Craters left by exploding shells from these interchanges can be seen in the vicinity.*

tween these two worlds, was formed by the weight of the Bushveld Igneous Complex lavas. By pushing down the middle of the Transvaal Sequence, they caused these rocks to pop up along the outer edge of the formation. The bottom layer of this sequence is the Black Reef Quartzite, which forms this massive, erosion-resistant wall. On top of the quartzites lies a layer of dolomitic limestone, known as the Malmani Dolomites.

Because of the way in which the Transvaal Sequence has been lifted up, the dolomite layer lies to the west of the quartzites, behind

Previous pages: *Once these slopes in Magoebaskloof were covered in montane grasses, with dense natural forests sheltered in the more secluded valleys and gorges. The industrialization of South Africa last century all but depleted its natural hard-wood resources and led to the destruction of many of the natural forests. The mines needed props to support shafts kilometres beneath the ground; the railways needed sleepers; the cities needed building materials, furniture, fuel and paper. In all the country's fast-growing mountain areas pine and eucalyptus trees were planted and today the country has a thriving timber industry.*

Below: *Just west of the quartzitic rocks that form the Transvaal Escarpment lies a band of softer dolomite. When water seeps through this rock it forms weak carbonic acid, which slowly eats into cracks. Spectacular potholes and caves are formed, such as the Sudwala Caves seen here. As it runs over the the cave roof and drips down, the water deposits 'icicles' of calcium carbonate, called stalactites. Where the drops hit the cave floor, stalagmites grow upwards, and when the two meet they form fantastical fluted columns.*

the higher crests of the escarpment. Rain water forms weak carbonic acid when it percolates through dolomite, eating out hollows like the Echo Caves and the Sudwala Caves. The Black Reef was laid down initially as beach-type deposits and was later metamorphosed by the tremendous heat of the same volcanic extrusions that thrust it upwards. The intermittent layers of dolomite are derived from the carbonate remains of tiny marine creatures that settled on the floor of a primeval sea once the period of sand deposition had ceased.

The Blyde River begins its life near Sabie and flows northwards past Pilgrim's Rest, under an arched stone bridge and onwards to the gorge and famous potholes at Bourke's Luck which have been bored into the dolomitic bedrock by the river's scouring action. The potholes are named after a prospector who correctly surmised that these natural wells would be ideal traps for heavy gold particles, washed out from surrounding gold-bearing veins.

The village of Pilgrim's Rest arose during the gold rush there in the 1870s, but after World War II the mines petered out and the historic village drifted into a prolonged sleep. Its brightly painted corru-

gated iron houses and shops, and the pretty gardens along the gurgling Blyde (happy) River now constitute a fully restored national monument. The Royal Hotel, however, never closed its doors; to satisfy thirsty miners a bar was brought up by ox wagon from Lourenço Marques (now Maputo), where it had begun its service to mankind as a church.

At God's Window one looks out over the sheer precipices and across the hazy, pale Lowveld bush a kilometre below – when the view is not obscured by the clouds that so often cling, shroud-like, to the soaring cliffs. Beginning at this viewsite, the Blyderivierspoort Hiking Trail wanders off down the valley of the Treur River among

Below: *From the top of the damp escarpment to the hot Lowveld floor a multitude of crops is cultivated: citrus fruits, paw-paws, bananas, avocado pears and nuts grow in the valley of the Letsitele River below Tzaneen, while on the cooler slopes above the town tea plantations lend an Oriental flavour to this exotic banquet.*

Previous pages: *Phragmites ('whistle' reeds) line the sandy banks of the Olifants River, where wild figs, river combretums and other large riverine forest trees arch over the water. This river divides the Kruger National Park into two basic vegetation zones: to the south is open grassland with clusters of acacia, marula and combretum trees, while to the hotter, drier north, mopane woodland runs on into the Limpopo River basin.*

Above: *A herd of impala stands alert on the banks of the Shingwidzi River, where they are most vulnerable to attacks by large predators. When disturbed while browsing or grazing in the open savanna, these graceful antelope can outrun a lion and usually outdistance even a sprinting cheetah.*

the wooded hills, branching off up side valleys past high waterfalls and otter-inhabited backwaters, to meet the Blyde River at Bourke's Luck. From here the trail hugs the rim of southern Africa's second deepest canyon, until one descends between the mighty walls of Swadeni. The 800-metre-high turrets of Mariepskop and the Three Rondavels loom over the entrance to the Blyde River Canyon, guarding one of the few passages through the fortress of the escarpment.

The Transvaal Sequence rests on a granite floor two billion years old which paves most of the Lowveld and forms the boulder koppies in the southern section of the Kruger National Park. The park preserves the quintessential spirit of old Africa, having been brought about by the word, the deed and the law of three far-sighted and determined men.

The Lowveld was the uncharted hunting ground of The South African Republic. Even then President Paul Kruger realized that in order for his grandchildren to see lion or kudu in the wilds, something decisive would have to be done to preserve this fast-vanishing heritage. In 1898 he proclaimed a 'Gouvernement Wildtuin' here,

Right above: *A king patrols his territory, claiming his royal dues and commanding respect from all other creatures in the African bush. A fully grown lion is a formidable carnivore, with immense power and lightning speed. Although lions usually avoid them, they are known on occasion to attack even elephants – although in such a case the lion may well end up dead.*

Right centre: *Klipspringers (meaning 'rock jumpers') are specifically adapted to living in rocky and mountainous terrain. In the Lowveld they stick to the granite koppies, where their padded, tip-toe hooves allow them to bounce over the rocks with astounding speed. They are, however, vulnerable to hunting as they usually stand and face a threatening presence – evolution has yet to equip them to escape bullets.*

Right: *The laws of ecology decree that in nature every available niche will be filled – and the African bush is perhaps the best place to observe this. From the smallest antelope to the lofty giraffe, every level of grazing and browsing is utilized by some species. Giraffes feed on plant resources beyond the reach of other large and small mammals.*

Above: *Dust in the winter bushveld skies creates of every sunset a bewitching extravaganza.*

later known as the Sabie Game Reserve. In 1902 Major Stevenson-Hamilton was appointed as the reserve's first guardian. He devoted the next forty-four years of his life to its protection and in the process became a living legend. Intervening wars and the dissent of local farmers and hunters did little to further conservation efforts in the Lowveld. In 1926, however, the Minister of Lands, Piet Grobler (one of Kruger's grandsons), pushed the National Parks Act through Parliament, proclaiming the Kruger National Park as its first ward.

The western strip of the Kruger Park is underlain by Old Granite and the eastern half composed of much younger Lebombo Basalts (of the Karoo's Stormberg Group). Rainfall decreases steadily from south to north. The broad ecosystems within the park are determined by the intersection of these two environmental gradients, modified by the seven main rivers that traverse the park from west to east.

The Olifants River more or less bisects the park, acting as a dividing line between the two main vegetation zones: mopane woodlands, studded with the massive forms of baobab trees, stretch over the deep, loamy soils north of the river; in the south-west mixed acacia and combretum savanna grows on the relatively poor granitic soils, while open grassland with scattered, large marula, acacia, knobthorn and umbrella thorn trees grow on the richer basaltic soils in the south-east.

Twenty species of antelope are found in the Kruger Park, all of which might be expected to compete for the same food resource. However, close observation reveals that each species occupies a slightly different niche. The delicate mouth of the steenbok requires it to nibble green shoots, while tsessebe will be found feeding in tall, coarse grasslands on the edge of woodlands. Impala will graze green grass and browse on seed pods, leaves and flowers, while the handsome roan depend entirely on medium to long grasses, especially red grass (*Themeda triandra*) in open woodlands.

Where there is prey, there will be predators. Like the antelope, the carnivores and scavengers have their own niches, with different favourite prey and different methods of hunting. While it would seem logical that the predators determine the numbers of prey that can survive in the park, in fact it is the other way around.

Lions are so powerful that they can bring down grown buffalo, but they often prefer to scavenge the kills of subordinate predators. Cheetahs have slight frames and rely on bursts of great speed to bring down small antelope. Cheetahs and wild dogs hunt in daylight, hyaenas and leopards are mainly nocturnal killers, while in different areas lions will hunt by night or day. Visitors to the park may see a kill, but early risers are often rewarded by seeing an early hunt or a pride of lions feeding on a fresh carcass, with spotted hyaenas and vultures in close attendance.

Sunrise is a fine time to be up and observant here: a line of bee-eaters may be illuminated, huddled together on a branch like a bejewelled brooch, before flitting off into the crisp air; the new day's sunlight sparkles on the dew-hung grass; animals stir and sniff the fresh breeze – this is dawn just as the first person would have experienced it.

Above: *In Africa the baobab is the king of trees. Their grotesque forms are found only in the lower, hotter areas of the Lowveld and along the northern border of the subcontinent. Carbon dating has revealed that the largest of these trees – those with a girth of about eight metres of more – may be as much as 3 000 years old. During droughts, elephants break off chunks of the fibrous trunks to chew the spongy wood.*

Northern Transvaal
and Highveld

The Magaliesberg range of mountains, which forms a narrow wild-life sanctuary between Pretoria, Rustenburg, Johannesburg and Krugersdorp, is a special and unique natural feature, although it can easily be overlooked as nothing more than a line of unimpressive hills. Its main attraction is that it is a small piece of African bush amid the subcontinent's largest and fastest-developing urban and industrial complex.

Deeply incised into its quartzitic scarps is a system of extensive gorges, with vertical sides reaching heights of up to 100 metres. A mixed Afro-montane, bushveld and riverine forest vegetation finds refuge here: large tree ferns thrive in the spray of the waterfalls that fill the kloofs with their music; wild fig trees send out showers of roots across the rock faces, spanning overhangs like the strings of huge harps; occasionally a flush of forest birds flits through the dappled canopies, while black eagles and Cape vultures, which nest on the cliff faces, and martial eagles soar high in the sky at the very limit of human vision.

Klipspringers and grey rhebuck are common in the rocky outcrops and open grasslands of summit grasslands, while brown hyaena, leopard and even the extremely rare pangolin or scaly ant-eater have been sighted here from time to time. The range's ecological significance is that it forms a link as well as a barrier between the temperate Highveld grasslands to the south, and the northern Bushveld savanna. Species from these two biomes co-exist here and form a unique mix.

The kloofs which invest the mountains with such unexpected diversity and fertility cut the tilted, metamorphosed rocks at intersecting angles of 60 and 120 degrees – the very same angles that deter-

Previous pages: *In the lee of the Magaliesberg, Haartebeestpoort Dam provides a recreational focus for the Pretoria-Johannesburg metropolis.*

Above: *Sun City, poised on the edge of the volcanic outcrop known as the Bushveld Igneous Complex, juxtaposes a glittering emporium of city temptations – such as golf, gambling and rock music concerts – with the African bushveld and Third World rural existence in the Bophuthatswana homeland.*

Right: *The Pilanesberg Game Reserve occupies a geological formation called an alkaline ring complex, of which this is the largest in the world. It is a circular rock formation created by the welling up of a volcanic cauldron.*

Previous pages: *Greater flamingoes in the Lichtenburg Nature Reserve form a chorus line in their gay pink plumage. Their goose-like call is usually issued in chorus, often by flocks numbering hundreds and even thousands of birds.*

Above: *An archetypal Highveld scene – wildebeest graze in the Suikerbosrand Nature Reserve. In the past 150 years, however, these scenes have all but vanished and the Transvaal Highveld is now a highly urbanized or cultivated area.*

mine the crystalline structure of quartzite, from which the mountains are composed. The fault lines which form these kloofs must be fractures that formed when the weight of the Bushveld Igneous Complex thrust up the surrounding rocks.

The Magaliesberg range was named after Chief Mohale who, with his tribe, sought refuge from Mzilikazi in its sheltering folds. On his bloody path to becoming king of the Matabele nation, the renegade Zulu chief Mzilikazi swept across the Transvaal interior early in the 19th-century, mercilessly conquering all the tribes he encountered *en route*. Playing his own significant part in the Difaqane Wars, Mzilikazi helped to devastate a pastoral existence that had thrived for centuries.

The geology of the Transvaal is very old and extremely complex, forming a jumbled mosaic of mineral types and topographical forms. They range from the earth's oldest Fundamental Complex sediments and intrusive granites, through the slightly younger but similar 'Dominion' rocks, gold-bearing 'Witwatersrand', the marginal 'Ventersdorp', the extensive 'Transvaal', to the very contorted 'Loskop' and overlying but undisturbed 'Waterberg' systems, and the oval magmas of the Bushveld Igneous Complex. Iron banding is characteristic of many of the older formations, a feature which was significant in determining much of the region's late pre-history.

Only scattered fragments of Karoo Supergroup rocks remain, most significantly the coal-bearing Ecca shales of the south-eastern Transvaal. Dwyka tillite, deposited by the melting glacier that heralded the onset of the Karoo depositional period, once lay over much of the Transvaal. The gently rolling valleys of the Vaal, Harts and middle Orange rivers were planed off by this ice flow. Nearly all of the Dwyka tillite has been removed by erosion, except in deep troughs of older rock beds.

In the centre of the province lies the heavy volcanic extrusion called the Bushveld Igneous Complex, which was dumped on top of the Transvaal Sequence sandstones of the Precambrian period. The great heat and weight of this igneous eruption metamorphosed the underlying strata to form glassy quartzites and, like a fist pressing down in the middle of a pliable mat, forced them up along its rim. The Magaliesberg range and the Eastern Transvaal Escarpment were formed in this manner.

The most recent fossil records and genetic research suggest that it was on the open grasslands of eastern and southern Africa that Man evolved from apes; more specifically it was from this area that modern man spread out to dominate the Neanderthals and other lesser branches of the *Homo* family tree. Iron Age ruins and artefacts from

successive indigenous dynasties can be found throughout the Highveld and northern Transvaal, as well as ancient mines which probe its ore-bearing hillsides. Stone ruins found in the Soutpansberg's foothills and in the Limpopo River Valley's sweltering mopane woodlands resemble those of Zimbabwe's famous remains. This suggests that the legendary golden empire of Monomatapa was extensive, long-lived and founded on iron and not gold at all.

From its incoming highways, and especially from the air, the reflecting planes of Johannesburg's highrise buildings loom out of the buff Highveld in anachronistic splendour. The entire Witwatersrand metropolis can be likened to the colony of some dominant, geometric-minded species of insect – a nuclear age termitarium. Like all other species that inhabit the earth, *Homo sapiens* will invariably succeed to another form, or exhaust its genetic capabilities and simply disappear. But massive concrete and metal structures may survive after their biological creators have returned to dust, monuments to another age ... the steel – or perhaps the gold – age.

Above: *White-breasted cormorants come home to roost at Barberspan Nature Reserve. Southern Africa is a basically dry region, and wetlands like this one are vital not only for the conservation of wildlife, but also for the supply of water to farms and cities. Pans and vlei's act as reservoirs for rainwater during wet seasons, and release their water slowly through the dry season. If they are filled in or drained, as so often happens, an area will be denied this supply.*

Botswana

Southern Africa's spectacular scenery is apparent mostly in its great expanses. Vistas of pastel bands stretch on and on in every direction and the shimmering glare welds the pale horizon to the eggshell sky. Nowhere does this openness seem as infinite as in the great sand basin of the Kalahari. Endless stretches of silver-dry grasses interspersed with camel thorn trees cover the 300-metre-thick mantle of sand. Sparsely vegetated oxidized-red dunes cover most of Bostwana like an old and tattered Bushman's jackal-skin karos, laid out for his bed.

Only occasionally do ancient granite hills protrude through the deep sand: at Otse in the country's south-east corner, for instance, where a small breeding colony of endangered Cape vultures is found; at Tsau in the central Kalahari and Kgwebe near Lake Ngami; the Chinamba and Gubatsha hills which flank the Mababe Depression in Chobe National Park; and, most impressively, beyond the northwestern corner of the Okavango Delta where the Tsodilo Hills

Previous pages: *The Okavango is an inland delta, set in the middle of the Kalahari sand basin. Once a year floodwaters from the Angolan highlands find their way down here along the Kavango River, and inundate this vast area. Only termite mounds and* Hyphaene *palms protrude above the level ground.*

Below: *After a hard day's eating (a fully-grown elephant consumes about 200 kilograms of grass and leaves every day), a herd of elephants descends on the Chobe River to drink and bathe.*

cast their mysterious shadows. In the late-1970s the !Kung Bushman clan, headed by Bo, one of the last great hunters living in the old way, still used these sacred hills as the hub of its extensive range. Paintings adorn the flaking, lichen-encrusted rock faces and cave walls and in all but the driest years water can be found trickling deep within a narrow crevice.

Almost unbelievably, to the east of these cracked hills the richest freshwater wetland system in Africa rests on the Kalahari's hot and spongy sands. Bostwana is essentially arid sand country, but rivers that rise in Angola's southern highlands hesitantly enter the Kalahari basin to soothe its sunburned brow. The water is disgorged into broad swamplands, creating contorted channels as it passes through filtering reed beds, which splay out across inland deltas braided with innumerable channels, countless identical islands and deep, cool lagoons; eventually dissipating into the fickle pans of Lake Ngami and Lake Xau.

African jacanas, using their long toes to hop from lily pad to lily pad, trot across the Okavango's hidden lagoons, pecking at seeds, insects and small crustaceans as they go. Red-billed teal and white-faced whistling ducks peel off in their hundreds for the sparkling aquamarine lakes. Pygmy geese with their green, white and rust-orange heads forage in the stagnant backwaters for insect larvae and the seeds of lotus lilies.

The ever-shifting channels of the river skirt around flat islands, almost always with a pyramidal termite mound in the centre surrounded by grass meadows, then a ring of tall *Hyphaene* palms and skirted by a ribbon of stout mahogany and motsaodi trees and the

buttressed trunks of sycamore figs and other riverine forest trees. Between open channels and islands there are thickets of papyrus and aquatic meadows of hippo grass. Herons, egrets and elegant saddlebill storks with their chunky black, red and yellow beaks stride through the shallows, picking at fish fry, frogs and crabs.

Fish eagles perch on *Hyphaene* palms, like Roman standards on top of ornate columns, waiting for bream or tiger fish to break the water surface. Having spotted its prey, a fish eagle swoops with its talons thrust out and snatches at the water, throwing up a crystal spray, then its fish-heavy undercarriage swings behind. With pumping wingbeats the majestic raptor slowly rises, primary feathers seeming to claw at the air, as it gains speed and height.

Undoubtedly the most fascinating bird of the freshwater wetlands is Pel's fishing owl. It is a buff-coloured, nocturnal bird that fishes in much the same way as fish eagles do. Conflict between these two large piscivores is avoided as the owls rest during the day in the crook between trunk and bough of the yellowish-white motsaodi trees, in the shadow of the larger forest species, while the fish eagles are active.

Miombo woodland, which covers the moister savanna to the

Right: *The Savuti Channel that connects the Okavango Delta to the Chobe River rarely flows, and is usually no more than a series of muddy puddles. But even these pools are vital for elephants, hippo, giraffe and the other game which occupy this temperamental land.*

north and east of the Okavango and Chobe area, just touches this area. The msasa and munondo woodlands with medium grass cover offer a suitable habitat for roan and sable antelope. Where the hot Kalahari sands sizzle on the edge of these wetlands, gemsbok and springbok graze among the mopane and camel thorn trees in the dusty Mababe Depression and towards the Tsodilo Hills to the west. Here the moist savanna and desert ranges of these antelope almost meet, separated only by a narrow ribbon of fragile wetlands in the midst of pervading aridity.

When Frederick Courtney Selous first went hunting elephant along the Chobe River in 1874, he wrote of 'teak forests' and 'impenetrable jungles' stretching back at least two kilometres from the water, slowly giving way to acacia thornveld and mopane woodlands. Since the 1870s the elbow of land between the Okavango Delta, Savuti Channel and Chobe River has drawn hunters in ever increasing numbers to a gallery that includes just about every species of game and bird found in southern Africa. Because of pressure from mushrooming human populations in the Caprivi, Zimbabwe and Botswana itself, 45 000 elephants have been compressed into the Chobe National Park, where the land's natural carrying capacity has been far exceeded.

This concentration of such large herbivores has had a disastrous effect on the area's vegetation, and small woodland game such as the Chobe bushbuck and beautiful Narina trogon have been driven out. The elephants have broken through the once-dense gallery forest along river's banks, and the flanking woodlands are now stripped and trampled.

The great sand mantle that smothers the Kalahari is the last refuge of the diminutive yellow hunters, who followed the rains across

Above: *On the flat expanses of Botswana, land and sky meet in endless vistas, either in the lagoons and river channels of the Okavango Delta, or the mirages that float upon the flanking salt pans.*

the subcontinent for longer than Bo's small clan can remember – and the collective memory of the Bushmen stretches back into the primal past. The !Kung of the northwest, the !Xo of the south and the /Gwi and Nharo clans of the central Kalahari speak quite different languages and do not share a common mythology and yet in appearance and in their hunter-gatherer lifestyles, they are indistinguishable.

Since the terrible drought of the early 1980s that ravaged the entire southern hemisphere, there are no more San people living naturally in the central Kalahari, for they have been forced out to live around government waterholes on the edge of the thirstland. Even their accumulated wisdom, their magic and resourcefulness could not withstand the heat and dryness that drove away all the game and sucked up every drop of water from the underground pools.

It was not an easy decision for these children of the 'great sandface' to relinquish their freedom or the excitement and fulfilment of the hunt. But modern times have not been kind to the Bushmen. Having barely survived a century of senseless persection, the ravages of other people's wars and an ever-advancing wave of pastoralists, they were finally cheated by the winds which once too often forgot to bring rain.

Anyone raised in a city would soon perish if left alone in the Kalahari, even if they were given all the material possessions of a Bushman. Meat is their most sought-after food, but although game is

Above: *A herd of buffalo moves over the seasonal swamplands of the Okavango – a confusing expanse of land and water: here one is never quite sure where the one begins and the other ends, or when the land will be under water.*

Above: *The delta region draws game to it from deep within the Kalahari wastelands, but it is the birdlife that makes this marvellous wetland such a wildlife paradise. On the upper reaches of the delta's permanent waterways, squacco herons come to roost in the papyrus beds near Shakawe. When not in flight these birds are shy and well-camouflaged, often standing quite still for long periods, and so are seldom seen.*

plentiful here, it is always on the move. Great 'magic' is needed to ensure a successful hunt. The Bushmen use small bows and light arrows, relying on poison to kill their large prey. First the poison must be collected and prepared, then the game must be located. Divining discs are used to determine when to begin the chase, and then a spoor must be picked up and followed.

When an animal is sighted it must be approached to within less than 50 metres – but a snapped twig or change in wind direction would eliminate hours or days of tiring work. The instant that an eland, gemsbok or giraffe has been hit, it will take off and must be tracked for as long as it takes the poison to work, which may be up to three days. When the divining discs reveal no signs of game, smaller prey will be sought, such as tortoises and pythons. Spring hares, aardvarks and warthogs will be speared in their burrows with long, flexible poles; ostrich eggs make an excellent omelette and are used for storing water along a group's hunting and gathering trails; a female hornbill and her chicks can be dug out from their clay-sealed nest in a hollow tree trunk.

The boys and men are experts are snaring small game and birds, the most sought-after of which is the stout kori bustard. The strong

Below: *Moremi Game Reserve lies on the eastern fringe of the Okavango Delta, making the most of permanent waterways, intermittent swamplands and the savanna woodlands of northern Botswana. Xakanaxa Lagoon is one of the largest of the delta's permanent lakes, and is famous for its heronries. Egrets and storks also nest there.*

Right: *This baobab is one of a group that stands on the edge of Nxai Pan, a dying lake that lies on the trade route followed by hunters and explorers such as John Andersson and Thomas Baines. Baines was an excellent artist who documented his travels in now-famous paintings, among which was a painting of this group of trees.*

Above: *Tranquillity hangs over the Linyanti River, unchanged from primeval days. If a paradise on earth still exists, then it must surely be the wetlands of northern Botswana.*

wings of this largest of all flying birds, say the Bushmen, fanned the great fire which was used to brand all the animals with their respective markings. While the men are expert hunters, it is the women who provide most of the daily sustenance. They spend their days fetching water, digging for succulent roots and tubers, collecting spiky cucumis and tsama melons and squash-like monkey oranges, picking brandybush berries and the protein-and-oil-rich mangetti nuts. Most covetted of all is honey, relished even more than baked giraffe brain or blood pudding made from an eland's stomach.

To the men falls the important task of collecting the dripping combs. Whenever the bird known as the honey guide is heard singing nearby, they drop whatever they are doing to follow it. Invariably it leads them to a hive, where the bees are subdued with smoke and the combs extracted with ease. There will always be a share left for the bird, for they believe that, if this is not done, the next time it will lead them to a honey badger's burrow – and no-one, not even a lion or pack of wild dogs wants to upset one of these small, tough

and fearless animals.

Against Kalahari black-maned lions the !Kung are more than evenly matched, but against the pressures of modern technology they have few defences. Bushmen have always loved tobacco, marula beer and marijuana, but boreholes and brandy have proved to be the more powerful narcotic. It seems that the gap between the natural harmony of these Late Stone Age innocents and the mechanical discord of the nuclear age was just too great for them to breach.

Their disappearance will surely be our loss, for with them will perish one of man's strongest intuitive links with nature. But Africa is an enduring place and even the era of the Bushmen is but a flicker in the life of a continent that has witnessed the birth of all terrestrial life. The stars at night are the fires of Bushmen hunters who have departed the earthly realm, and now wander across the skies; our forms will forever change, but the energy remains constant to generate new life. This is the way it has always been, knowledge of which has allowed the Bushmen to accept their fate with stoicism and dignity.

Above: *In the vastness of the Okavango swamps, it is easy to overlook nature's more gentle artistry, as seen in this delicate pink flower among the reeds.*

Zimbabwe

An ancient lake once cast a vast mass of cool water over the Kalahari's deep sand mantle. It was the largest lake the world has seen and was fed by the many rivers that flowed into this huge basin. Then the earth belched and a seismic wave rose to disturb the shallow lake's tranquil surface. All along its trembling shoreline, birds took off in fright; hippos in the water bellowed in alarm at this invisble enemy that shook the very foundation of their world. The tremors continued for some time, causing animals to mill around in trepidation, not knowing in which direction to flee. Then the shudders subsided and the silt settled in the lake, but the earthquake that was centred beneath Lake Makgadikgadi had rearranged its drainage channels, diverting south-flowing rivers to the east, and draining much of the giant lake forever.

An old line of weakness was revealed, long forgotten since a 100-million-year-long period of volcanic activity had beset eastern and southern Africa. During this time the Karoo and Lebombo lavas were spewed out; the Great Rift Valley was torn open; as extensions of this continental fault the Zambezi and Limpopo mobile belts were stretched out, collapsed and their troughs partially filled with basalt.

The Zambezi River rises in the highlands of Zambia and Angola, and aeons ago it flowed southwards across the Barotse Plain to fan out into vast Lake Makgadikgadi. Then the lake's arteries were severed and the mighty river wandered off down the old tectonic faultline, moving eastwards in search of the Indian Ocean. Once past the sandy bed of the Barotse Plain, the river entered the Zambezi Trough and spread its waters out across the basalt pavement, braiding it with channels and islands. Its swiftly flowing waters carry a large load of sediment, the cutting tool of a patient sculptor. Along its course a fault crack was found and the river began, with its sediment, gradually to wear a vertical gap in the bedrock.

As the churning waters sliced deeper into the rock, the crack widened and deepened to form a 130-metre-deep chasm, into which cascaded the great sluice of water. Still the rushing waters eroded back along new faults, cutting diagonally back across the river until the falls were captured by a new gorge. It is possible today to identify eight interleading gorges below the Victoria Falls, over which the Zambezi River has plunged at various stages of its energetic retreat. It appears that the river has now found a new line of weakness to exploit, at the western extremity of the falls. Over the next few million years, the present chink in Devil's Island will develop into a second line of falls, until eventually it may absorb the entire flow.

During peak floods through March and April, the volume of water pouring over Victoria Falls increases some thirty-fold, when it becomes impossible to see the entire two-kilometre-wide chasm. The best time to appreciate the falls is in the late afternoon or at full moon when the water is low. The beguiling light casts rainbows within the spray, throwing a spectral arch over *Mosi o Thunya* – 'the smoke that thunders'. Within the rainforests that are fed by the mists of the waterfall, rather than real rain, sycamore figs, ebony, waterberry and wild olive trees attain impressive stature.

Previous pages: *Above the Victoria Falls the Zambezi River spreads out across a wide basalt bed, deep and calm, with no indication of the thundering spectacle that follows.*

Left: *The Zambezi River plunges 130 metres into the gorge below across a two-kilometre-wide sweep. During the course of its journey through the Zambezi trough faultline, the river has cut eight gorges into the volcanic bedrock and appears now to be cutting a ninth: the jet of water called the Devil's Cataract, over which a rainbow arches in this picture, is eroding a new gorge back from the present line of falls.*

Above: *The Eastern Cataract of the Victoria Falls, seen in one of its quieter states. When in flood the quantity of water spilling over this wide lip increases about thirty-fold. At this time the falls are obscured by a cloud of billowing mist, from which comes its local name of* Mosi o Thunya *– the smoke that thunders.*

Previous pages: *After passing through the many gorges before and after Kariba Dam, the Zambezi River spreads out over a wide floodplain before leaving Zimbabwe to pass through Mozambique to the sea. Due to deposition of silt on this plain, the river is moving its channel steadily northwards, leaving behind the 0x-bow lakes and smaller ponds of Mana Pools.*

Above: *At World's View in the Inyanga mountains, one stands near to the country's highest point – Inyanga Peak.*

Most of Zimbabwe consists of the central Matabele Highveld. These rolling uplands dip away to the west into the flat plain of the Kalahari sandveld, while along its eastern frontier the land rises up into the Inyanga, Vumba and Chimanimani mountain chain. To the north the highlands recede into the Zambezi Trough, where the river flows through a series of deep gorges or meanders over a wide floodplain. To the south the country descends into the broader depression of the Limpopo River. These two oppressively hot lowlands are formed by the fault lines of two parallel mobile belts. The entire country has been re-exposed over the past 150 million years by erosion of the vast bed of Karoo sandstones and shales, that remain only in a small pocket of coal-bearing rocks in the Hwange district.

The Eastern Highlands are an interlinked extension of the Great Escarpment. Their origins are somewhat vague, and they are estimated at between 2 800 and 2 000 million years old. The high peaks and ridges of the Inyanga and Chimanimani mountains consist of sheared and folded sugary-white quartzite, cut through by black doleritic bands. Near Mutare the southerly Chimanimanis are shifted to the east along a fault. Where the two ranges are disconnected, the Vumba mountains rise up between them as part of the underlying base of granite. With the exceptions of Frontier and Karoo outcrops, just about all of Zimbabwe's surface is composed of Primitive Granite, surrounded by bands of even older Fundamental Complex schists, to form large landscape cells. Along the circumference of these cells the granite forms massive convex shields, from which the weathering rock breaks away like peeling skin. Within the cells, one finds the characteristic castle-koppies, where balls of orange rock stand one upon the other, ponderously balancing on larger domes.

The Motoba Hills near Bulawayo are the best and by far the most spectacular example of these formations where, among others, Mzilikazi and Cecil John Rhodes lie buried. To the Kananga people who lived here until massacred by the first king of the Matabele, these rounded hills were the 'Malindizumu' – the dwelling place of the spirits. The Motobas were named by Mzilikazi, who jokingly called them 'Ama toba' – the bald heads of his indunas. The spirit of the Bushmen lives on here: magnificent examples of their rock art can be seen in the large caves that pock the hills. Today these hills are one of the country's prime wildlife sanctuaries. Apart from big game in the surrounding bush, they hold the densest concentrations of leopard and black eagle, which are well fed by the abundance of small antelope, baboons and rock hyraxes that thrive here.

The long sedimentary geological periods were followed by volcanic upheaval which generated severe internal stresses. The Bushveld Igneous Complex was pushed up in the Transvaal, while a huge crack was opened up in the basal granite of Zimbabwe and then filled in with molten rock from the same source. Subsequent erosion has left a raised spine of volcanic rock running from south to north across the country, just off centre, culminating in the Umvukwe mountains. It is called the Great Dyke and is the largest such intrusion known. Like the Bushveld Igneous Complex, it is composed of metal-rich ores from which high quality chrome, gold, nickel, as-

Above: *The Mtarazi Falls plunge over the Inyanga mountains in eastern Zimbabawe. These mountains, and the Chimanimani mountains to the south are formed by a ridge of course-grained quartzite and dolerite bands that rest on top of basement granite. While the quarzites have been dated from between two and 2,8 billion years ago, the granite basement is a few hundred million years older still!*

Above: *The skeletons of a mopane forest that was drowned by the rising waters of Lake Kariba. At the time it was built, in the mid-1950s, Lake Kariba was the largest man-made dam in the world. Today it is but one of many hydro-electric dams that have been built on southern Africa's major rivers.*

bestos and platinum are mined. During its long period of cooling, the heavier minerals settled out from the lighter ones, resulting in a wavey, banded wall 500 kilometres long and varying between three and 12 kilometres wide.

Above: *A glowing sunset casts warm colours over 'Starvation Island', and the waters of Lake Kariba.*

Along the north-eastern border of Zimbabwe, the Zambezi River flows out across the wide floodplain, with park-like terraces receding to low escarpments on both sides of the lazy river. The terraces reveal how the river has pushed its channel slowly northwards across the geological trough. Miombo woodland with its dominant msasa (*Brachystegia*) trees grows on the higher ground, while dense mopane scrub with the occasional baobab replaces it on the hotter, lower slopes. Along the floodplain the gaping, rubbery mouths of hippopotamuses have cropped the flat grasslands to resemble lawns. On this open savanna, ana trees (*Acacia albida*) grow up to 30 metres high while along the river banks mahogany and sausage trees spread their filigree crowns.

White sandbanks edge the river, upon which crocodiles bask in fossilized stupor; hippos appear like rocks in the river, their huge heads occasionally breaking the surface as they bellow with cavernous mouths agape and crowbar tusks flashing. Local fishermen in dugout canoes negotiate the shifting channels over ghostly, sinuous shoals. At Mana Pools, large ox-bow lakes and many smaller pools have been formed on the flood terraces. The river has made tight loops on the floodplain and then migrated on its north-bound course to leave the typical horseshoe-shaped pools. Every year the river comes down in flood and flushes out these pools, depositing new layers of rich mud and leaving fish and small aquatic animals stranded.

During the wet season when the flood plain becomes inundated, the big game in Mana Pools National Park keep to the higher woodlands. As the waters subside and the plain dries out, the animals and large wading birds appear to eat the flush of food that has been delivered by the floods. During the rainless winter months, the 12 000 elephants that live in the park seldom move far away from the river. They eat grass and leaves by stripping the ana trees of branches to about six metres above the ground.

Towards the end of winter the ana trees are adorned with bright

orange and reddish-brown curly seed pods. These nutritious fruits give the trees their local name of apple-ring thorn trees and they are much relished by game, for whom food has now become scarce. At this time elephants can be seen knocking the trees to obtain the pods. They rock the tall stems until a whiplash action brings the pods raining down. Impala herds and baboon troops tag after the pachyderms to feed on the surplus windfall of pods.

Between the chasm of Victoria Falls and the flattened valley at Mana Pools, Lake Kariba spreads out as far as an inland sea. Its secret waters hide a once-fearsome gorge wherein dwelt the river god 'Nyaminyami', and hilly bush country that stretched before the Matusadona mountains. The flat-topped Bumi Hills lie on the edge of the lake and march beneath its concealing surface. Some of the higher hill tops protrude to form small islands. Lions are known still to exercise their territorial rights over these hills by swimming from the mainland for several kilometres between the islands.

When Kariba Dam was completed in the early 1950s, its rising waters drowned a mopane forest whose stark forms loom out of the shallows along the shores of Matusadona National Park. Elephants like to feed on the lush grass along the waterline and to wade in shallow bays. They seem to drift between mopane trunks like ghostly galleons, as they scoop up the juicy stems and floating bulbs of aquatic plants.

During the day the liquid cooing of doves bubbles out from the wooded hills; the arrogant cry of fish eagles resonates across the lake as they swoop above its depths and settle on the outstretched limbs of the drowned trees. At sunset the eagles fly off to nest in the fringing hills and flights of water birds arrive to take their place. Cormorants and darters ruffle their wings and shake the last droplets of water from their oily feathers. The descending sun throws a shimmering film across the lake and melts over the grey-green hills of Zambia like a blob of hot wax. Herons and wood ibises tuck their heads into downy clefts between wing and breast, as the last flame-flecks of dying sunlight are doused in the lake.

Left: *Yellow-billed egrets bustle about elephants on the Zambezi floodplain like attendants on royalty. They feed mainly on fish and amphibians, but here they benefit from the small animals that are disturbed by the elephants' drinking and bathing.*

Above: Gnidia kraussiana *flowering in the Inyanga mountains. These plants, and many others that grow along Africa's eastern and southern mountain archipelago, are related to the Cape fynbos flora.*

Index